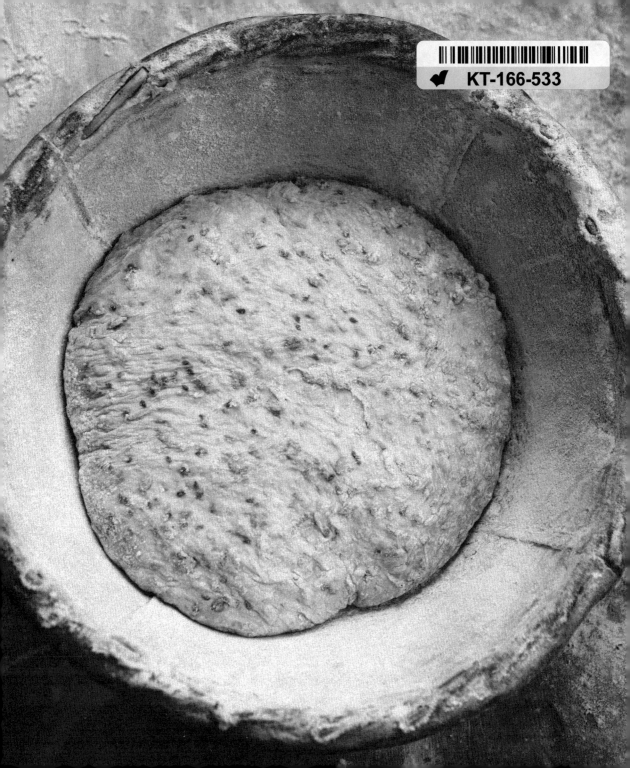

panini

EXPRESS

panini
EXPRESS

*70 delicious recipes,
hot off the press*

daniel leader &
lauren chattman

photography by ellen silverman

The Taunton Press

To Octavia, for not giving up the fight

Text © 2008 by Daniel Leader & Lauren Chattman
Photographs © 2008 by Ellen Silverman

The Taunton Press
Inspiration for hands-on living®

The Taunton Press, Inc., 63 South Main Street, PO Box 5506, Newtown, CT 06470-5506
e-mail: tp@taunton.com

Editor: Pamela Hoenig
Copy Editor: Karen Fraley
Proofreader: Patricia Jalbert-Levine
Indexer: Heidi Blough
Jacket/Cover Design: Alison Wilkes
Interior Design & Layout: Leah Carlson-Stanisic
Photographer: Ellen Silverman
Photo Assistant: Christina Holmes
Food Stylist: Susan Spungen
Prop Stylist: Betty Alfenito

Library of Congress Cataloging-in-Publication Data
Leader, Daniel.
 Panini express : 70 delicious recipes, hot off the press / Daniel Leader and Lauren Chattman.
    p. cm.
 Includes index.
 ISBN 978-1-56158-960-9
 1. Sandwiches. 2. Cookery, Italian. I. Chattman, Lauren. II. Title. III. Title: Panini express, seventy delicious recipes,
hot off the press.

TX818.L43 2008
641.8'4--dc22
                        2007030109

Printed in Singapore
10 9 8 7 6 5 4 3 2 1

Acknowledgments

We would like to thank the following people for their crucial help in putting together this book: Angela Miller, a great agent and friend; Sharon Burns, for testing and retesting the panini; Octavia Fleck, for her many valuable suggestions and help in testing the recipes; Jack Bishop, for some great ideas and spot-on opinions; Susan Spungen, for incredible food prep and styling for the photo shoot; Sarah Bruno, for her hard work in gathering and preparing the food for the photo shoot; Ellen Silverman, for the timeless photos—I love every one of them; photo assistant Christina Holmes, for helping with the photos; Carrie Wolf at Jarden Consumer Solutions for providing the Villaware panini press that made all the panini for the photo shoot; Alison Wilkes, for her art direction of the photo shoot and the design of the book; Leah Carlson-Stanisic, for a design that brings out the simple beauty of the food; Kathleen Williams, for seeing the book safely through production; Katie Benoit, for pulling everything together; Pam Hoenig, for putting together such a terrific team and producing a breathtakingly beautiful book. Thanks again.

Contents

2 quick *mayonnaises, pestos,* and other sandwich *enhancers*

3 the *sandwiches*

Introduction

When I left my job as a chef in New York City to open my Catskills bakery 20 years ago, it was to simplify my life. Instead of making fancy food, I baked bread, trying to duplicate the delicious loaves I had tasted in Paris as a culinary student and had enjoyed as much as the lavish meals I had eaten at the city's Michelin-starred restaurants.

In the early years of my business, I traveled to France many times to learn more about how to make authentic French baguettes and boules. Legendary bakers including Bernard Ganauchaud, Eric Kayser, and Basil Kamir generously shared their techniques and recipes with me, but they also shared something else: sandwiches that they made for themselves, using freshly baked bread and a few simple ingredients—cheese, ham, mustard, mayonnaise. Occasionally we ate them at room temperature, but more often we grilled our sandwiches on the panini press that invariably sat behind the bakery counter. A warm sandwich, like a warm loaf of bread, is irresistible. The hot iron grids toast and refresh the bread so that it gives off that just-baked aroma. Warmed, the fillings are intensely flavorful and delicious.

I saw that Parisian bakers also sold these sandwiches to customers in need of a quick bite as well as a baguette. In the morning, bakery workers would pile up hundreds of sandwiches, Brie and *jambon cuit* (similar to our boiled ham), Gruyère and *jambon de Bayonne* (like Italian prosciutto), and other variations on the Croque Monsieur, and grill them to order throughout the day. Even at bakeries where this wasn't the practice, you didn't have to look far to find a sandwich. Next door to the world-famous Poilane, which only sold bread, was Cuisine du Bar, a café whose menu consisted exclusively of sandwiches made with bread from the bakery—combinations like baby artichokes and black olive tapenade; sheep's milk cheese, ham, and sun-dried tomatoes; grilled sardines and greens. Although I had named my business "Bread Alone," it wasn't long before I bought an imported sandwich press and started offering my version of the Croque Monsieur alongside my own breads.

After a few years of baking French breads exclusively, I decided to expand my repertoire to include breads from Italy, Germany, Austria, and Eastern Europe. I took dozens of short trips to these countries whenever I had a few free days, exploring them bakery by bakery, collecting recipes and learning techniques. Everywhere I went, I saw sandwiches alongside the breads. At the famous Campo di Fiori bakery, where I learned to make Roman-style pizza, I ate a sandwich of anchovies, arugula, chopped cherry tomatoes, and lemon vinaigrette on a fresh piece of focaccia. In Munich, I toured Tobias Maurer's bakery, where he makes dozens of types of whole-grain seeded breads, and noted that he had an entire room devoted to making sandwiches. I sampled one of smoked salmon and herb mayonnaise on pumpernickel as workers packed hundreds more in little plastic boxes to be delivered to Tobias's retail stores around the city. In a bakery high in the Swiss Alps, my friend Clemens Walsch made little rye rolls, which we then used to make grilled sandwiches of air-dried beef and Emmenthaler cheese. I returned to the Catskills after these trips with new bread recipes and new ideas for sandwiches to add to my café menu.

The sandwiches that European bakers make are as different as a loaf of whole rye is from a bubbly ciabatta. But whether it is Appenzell and caramelized onions on rye in the Swiss Alps, or a chicken sandwich with tarragon mayonnaise and red grapes on a baguette

in southern France, a baker's sandwich exhibits a special touch. It always consists of the smallest number of high-quality ingredients necessary for a tasty sandwich. The ingredients are sensitively handled and carefully arranged, so that they unite between the toasted bread in a neat and harmonious way. The result is like a good loaf, elemental and satisfying, and elegant in its simplicity.

Typically in European bakery cafés, only a few kinds of sandwiches are offered, always traditional combinations made with local ingredients. Parisians expect to see a Croque Monsieur on the menu and Florentines expect a *panino* filled with prosciutto and provolone. My diverse group of customers, in contrast, is interested in flavors from around the world, and I try to satisfy everyone. At Bread Alone, we offer a tuna and cheddar melt alongside a grilled corned beef and Muenster sandwich. I've been influenced by the tastes of the Mexican-American bakers who work here, so also I serve sandwiches filled with guacamole, fresh salsa, and grilled chicken. After my daughter returned from study in the Middle East, she cooked dishes with lamb, eggplant, feta cheese, and other tasty ingredients from that region; those components eventually wound up in Bread Alone sandwiches. But no matter what kind of sandwich I'm making, I try very hard to stick to the minimalist approach of my baker mentors, resisting my mad chef's urge to add another layer of cheese, an extra garnish, or another unnecessary frill.

In the last few years, the home panini press has taken its place alongside the toaster and blender as a must-have small appliance. Americans have discovered the pleasures of making their own perfectly grilled sandwiches. These machines grill sandwiches evenly in less time and with less mess than is possible on top of the stove. This book is for people who want to use the panini press to make sandwiches in the European bakery style. There are recipes here for a grilled Italian tuna and caper sandwich similar to one in Sicily and another for a corned beef and Muenster cheese sandwich like the one I had in Prague. But there are also sandwiches made with smoked turkey, avocado, and Indian-spiced tomato chutney or with chickpeas and the Middle Eastern spice mix zatar. I've tried hard to combine ingredients in natural and pleasing ways. There are no odd fusions of, say, Caribbean and Japanese elements, or any other attempts to be creative. I prefer filling ingredients that make sense together, so that my sandwiches are comforting and familiar instead of shocking or weird.

Bakers make sandwiches with ingredients on hand. No baker I know would insist on roasting his own chicken before making a chicken sandwich. So every recipe in this book is made with ingredients that you can buy at the supermarket or specialty foods store or prepare quickly at home, often in the time it takes the sandwich press to heat. The ease with which you can arrive at a wonderfully warm, aromatic, and delectable grilled sandwich is no small part of the appeal. You will truly be amazed at how little work and time it takes to produce such a sandwich, if you take just a little care in shopping for the right ingredients and putting them together.

Tips for Panini Press Success

You don't have to go to cooking school to make a grilled sandwich, but you do need to pay attention to the little things if you want it to be truly memorable. Here are a few tips, gleaned from my own experience at the bakery and at home, that I've found make the difference between an okay sandwich and a great one.

Choose the Right Press

The professional press I use at the bakery is imported from Italy, and similar to the presses I saw 20 years ago in Europe. It is very heavy, with thick iron grids that have become well-seasoned after years of use, which means the sandwiches don't stick. It has a temperature control, which I keep at 350 degrees, the right temperature for toasting, not burning, bread.

When I was buying a home press, I looked for one with similar capabilities. There are at least a dozen sandwich makers on the market right now, priced from $29 to over $100. You get what you pay for and, in general, the presses that cost more are heavier and more solidly constructed, and heat more evenly than the cheaper models. There should be a temperature gauge for controlling the heat. Look for models with a nonstick surface and a floating lid, which allows the machine to accommodate very thick sandwiches. Bigger surface area is better if you plan to grill more than one sandwich at a time. Some presses come with a special implement to help you clean between the grids without scratching the nonstick surface, a feature I highly recommend after having tried to clean my first press using balled-up paper towels and cotton swabs.

Buy or Bake Quality Bread

When you are grilling a sandwich, you need bread that has substance. Avoid the light, airy, fluffy bread produced by most commercial bakeries. This kind of bread doesn't grill well, becoming flattened and dry when pressed under the heavy lid of a sandwich maker. For the best sandwiches, use a European-style hearth bread made at a local bakery. These breads will be sturdy enough and moist enough to maintain their character as they are grilled.

Alternatively, try some of the simple bread recipes in Chapter 1, which I've designed especially for grilled sandwiches. These are straightforward breads made with packaged yeast, requiring a minimum amount of time to make from start to finish. Yet they are similar to some of the best sandwich breads in Europe. The Pizza Bread is made with dough similar to that used to make Roman pizza in the Campo di Fiori. The Seeded Focaccia has

the same mix of soaked seeds that many of Tobias Maurer's finest breads contain. The Four-Hour Baguettes are adapted from a standard French recipe often used by bakers for sandwiches. The fresh, yeasty scent of simple homemade bread will contribute to the wholesome goodness of any sandwich you make.

Think about Your Fillings

The best sandwich fillings have just the right balance of textures and flavors. Heavy meats and cheeses should be used in moderation. People in France and Italy would be shocked at the deli sandwiches often served here stuffed with 12 ounces of pastrami. Such large quantities don't stay neatly put between the slices of bread, making a sandwich ungainly and difficult to eat. To balance the richness of meats and melted cheese and to add textural interest to a sandwich, I often add a layer of soft-cooked vegetables such as grilled zucchini, mushrooms, or onions. They can add moisture without a lot of extra fat.

On sandwiches without cheese, I like a little mayonnaise or olive oil to bind the ingredients together and moisten the bread. But I rarely brush the outsides of the bread with oil or softened butter. The nonstick surface of my home panini press makes this unnecessary, and doing so makes a sandwich messy to pick up.

I enjoy my sandwiches even more if their ingredients look pretty together. A layer of sliced tomatoes or baby spinach will give a grilled cheese sandwich color as well as flavor. Red Pepper–Garlic Mayonnaise and Watercress Mayonnaise will do the same thing for a turkey or roast beef sandwich. When designing your own sandwich, think about pleasing visual contrasts as well as flavor and texture combinations. With a little planning, it is simple to construct a sandwich to please all of your senses.

The Golden Rule

With a few exceptions, most sandwiches benefit from a nice, long grilling. It can take up to 8 or 9 minutes, depending on how hot your press gets and how thick your sandwich is, for the interior to become thoroughly warmed and the bread to become deliciously caramelized. Don't be afraid to leave your sandwich on the grill until the bread becomes beautifully golden with reddish-brown grill marks. The temperature control of my home press is fixed at the high end, because I have found that at lower settings the bread dries out before the filling is adequately heated. But your press may be different. Play with the heat settings on your machine to discover the right one for a perfectly heated and toasted sandwich.

1
bread basics, basic breads

As a baker, of course I believe that quality bread is crucial to the success of any sandwich. Handmade hearth breads made by bakers schooled in European artisan bread-baking techniques have superior texture and flavor. These breads have a springy, moist crumb that won't dry out when toasted. They are sturdy enough to hold abundant fillings without falling apart. In contrast, commercial white and wheat breads made in a factory have a dry crumb and flabby crust. These breads will tear or turn to dust in the panini press. Hearth breads made with minimally processed flour and raised with a natural starter rather than commercial yeast lend a wholesome wheaty taste and delicious fermented aroma to sandwiches. Commercial bread is tasteless at best. Texture and flavor aside, artisan breads made with stone-ground organic flour are more nutritious than commercial bread made with industrially milled flour. The gentler milling process allows both white flour and whole wheat flour to retain the healthful oils and some or all of the bran that industrial milling entirely strips away.

In the past 20 years, American bakers schooled in European artisan techniques have spread out across the country, opening bakeries in large urban areas and in small towns. There is probably a bakery not far from your home where you can buy delicious handmade breads of all kinds to suit your sandwich needs. If not, you can probably buy great breads trucked to your supermarket or specialty foods store from a bakery farther afield. Breads made with natural starters have a long shelf life and will stay fresh for up to a week, so if you've always wanted to try bread from a particular bakery far from home, you can try ordering it online. If you can't get to Paris for *pain Poilane,* for example, you can have it delivered overnight, and enjoy the large loaf for several days after it arrives (see Resources, page 138). Bread freezes beautifully so, wherever you shop, buy several loaves at a time and freeze them for when you need them. They will keep for at least 2 weeks, wrapped tightly in plastic wrap or stored in zipper-lock bags.

There are no hard-and-fast rules for choosing a certain type of bread for a particular type of sandwich. Sometimes practicality will dictate the choice. A long piece of sausage fits comfortably inside a baguette that's the same length, but is awkward to position in a round pizza bread. A thin layer of melted cheese and a scattering of sautéed mushrooms might get lost inside two substantial slices of country bread, but will be just right inside a flatbread. But more often, choosing a particular bread for a sandwich is largely a matter of taste. I like my tarragon chicken salad on a ciabatta roll, but you might prefer it between slices of an eight-grain loaf. In every sandwich recipe, I suggest a type of bread that I like. But there is no reason why you can't substitute another bread that suits you better.

I began making pressed sandwiches with the loaves from my bakery, but as I worked on recipes for this book I thought it would be fun to develop some simple breads in the same spirit as the sandwiches, breads that are easy to make and don't require a whole lot of kitchen experience or a large investment of time. The bread recipes in this chapter are all made with packaged yeast and take no more than a few hours (and in some cases as little as one hour) from start to finish.

That's not to say that they are in any way a compromise. All of my experience as a baker has gone into creating these breads. So you will see that there is a lot of water in the ciabatta dough, a formula I picked up from Italian bakers for making a moist and bubbly bread. I caution against overkneading the flatbread dough, which will overdevelop the gluten and make it difficult to roll into large, thin rounds. Soaking the seeds before adding them to the Seeded Focaccia dough is a trick I learned in Germany to prevent the bread from drying out as it bakes. I'm really excited about the Grilled Pizza Bread recipe, because it is made from a dough similar to that used by the legendary Bartocci cousins at their Campo di Fiori bakery in Rome. Rather than baking the dough in a superheated oven (which results in a very crisp crackerlike crust), I stretch the dough over the grids of the panini press and briefly grill it until it is chewy but yielding—just right for sandwiches.

I hope you will give one of these recipes a try, even if you've never baked bread before. There is a lot of pleasure to be had from such simple recipes, and the results may even make you curious about bread recipes using natural starters or sponges instead of packaged yeast. I would be delighted if these breads became your stepping-stones to some of the truly great European artisan breads, such as *pain au levain,* or the Poilane-style whole wheat *miche* that I have discussed in my earlier books.

You'll need just a few ingredients to make these breads, so take care that they're of the best quality. I call for unbleached all-purpose flour because it has a similar protein content to the flour used by bakers in Europe. I highly recommend organic flour, which I believe encourages a higher rise and produces more flavorful bread. It is available at most natural foods stores and many supermarkets, and by mail (see Resources, page 138). Sea salt such as French fleur de sel also adds great flavor to bread. Take care when buying yeast. I specify instant yeast, which doesn't need to be dissolved in water before being mixed into dough. This is different from "fast-rising" yeast, which contains additives that will give bread an off-flavor.

Most of the recipes make more than enough bread for two sandwiches. Wrap leftover bread in plastic or put it in a zipper-lock bag and freeze for up to 2 weeks until you are ready to make more sandwiches.

CIABATTA Rolls

These simple rolls are the perfect shape for pressed sandwiches, with a crisp crust and an interior that's soft but not so thick and cottony that it will compete with the filling ingredients. If you'd like to flavor the rolls with fresh herbs, stir 1 tablespoon chopped fresh basil, parsley, oregano, or cilantro into the dough with the other ingredients. Use just 1 teaspoon of fresh rosemary, since it's more powerful than the others. If you know you are going to freeze the rolls, consider baking them for a shorter period—just until they are light golden. Then when you are ready to use them, put the frozen rolls in a preheated 350 degree oven for 10 minutes to finish the baking.

¾ cup plus 1 tablespoon (180 grams/6.35 ounces) tepid water (70 to 78 degrees)

1 teaspoon (5 grams/.2 ounce) instant yeast

1½ cups plus 2 tablespoons (250 grams/8.8 ounces) unbleached all-purpose flour

¾ teaspoon (5 grams/.2 ounce) sea salt or kosher salt

¾ teaspoon (5 grams/.2 ounce) granulated sugar

2½ tablespoons (28 grams/1 ounce) olive oil, plus more for oiling the pan and brushing the rolls

Pour the water into the bowl of a stand mixer fitted with a dough hook. Add the yeast, flour, salt, sugar, and olive oil and stir with a rubber spatula just long enough to blend into a dough. With the dough hook, mix the dough on low speed (2 on a KitchenAid® mixer) for 3 minutes. Turn the speed to medium-high (8 on a KitchenAid mixer) and knead until it clears the sides of the bowl and collects on the hook, becoming smooth and elastic, about 8 minutes more. At this speed, the mixer will "walk," possibly off the counter, so do not leave it unattended.

(Alternatively, in a food processor combine the yeast, flour, salt, and sugar and pulse 2 or 3 times to combine. With the motor running, pour the water and oil into the feed tube and process until the dough forms a smooth ball. To knead, continue to process for 30 seconds.)

Oil a 7 x 11-inch baking dish. Scrape the dough into the dish and pat it with oiled fingertips to flatten it. Let it rest and relax for 5 minutes, then use lightly oiled fingertips to push and stretch it across the bottom of the dish. Cover with plastic wrap and let the dough rise in a warm, draft-free spot until it has more than doubled in volume and reaches the top of the pan, about 2 hours.

Lightly oil a large baking sheet. Uncover the dough and place the baking sheet, right side down, on top of the dough. Invert the dish onto the baking sheet and shake once or twice to release the dough onto the sheet.

Use a sharp chef's knife to cut the dough into 6 squares, and use the edge of the knife to push the squares 3 inches apart on the baking sheet. Put 4 short drinking glasses near the corners of the pan and drape a sheet or two of plastic wrap over them so that it covers the dough pieces and keeps them moist but does not touch them. Let the dough pieces stand until they have expanded by about 50 percent, about 40 minutes.

Preheat the oven to 475 degrees. Remove the plastic and glasses and bake the rolls until dark golden brown, about 20 minutes. Brush the hot rolls with olive oil. Let cool completely on the baking sheet before slicing with a sharp serrated knife.

Grilled PIZZA BREADS

MAKES 2 FLATBREADS, ENOUGH FOR 2 SANDWICHES OR 2 INDIVIDUAL PIZZAS

These breads, made with my favorite pizza dough, are cooked right in the sandwich maker. They are chewy but tender rather than crisp, well seasoned with olive oil and sea salt. You can knead in some fresh herbs and/or up to 1 cup of grated Parmesan cheese to customize their flavor if you'd like. (For whole wheat pizza breads, substitute whole wheat flour for the all-purpose, and add an extra 2 tablespoons of water.) The dough is very wet, so use an electric mixer or food processor rather than kneading by hand, and don't be alarmed if bits of it are still sticking to the sides of the bowl when you are done. It will firm up enough to work with as it rises.

> ¾ cup plus 1 tablespoon (180 grams/6.35 ounces) tepid water (70 to 78 degrees)
>
> 1 teaspoon (5 grams/.2 ounce) instant yeast
>
> 2 tablespoons (25 grams/.9 ounce) olive oil
>
> 1½ cups plus 2 tablespoons (250 grams/8.8 ounces) unbleached all-purpose flour
>
> 1½ teaspoons (10 grams/.4 ounce) sea salt or kosher salt

Pour the water into the bowl of a stand mixer fitted with a dough hook. Add the yeast, oil, flour, and salt and stir with a rubber spatula just long enough to blend into a dough. With the dough hook, mix the dough on medium-high speed (8 on a KitchenAid mixer) for 8 to 10 minutes. The dough will look shiny but will still be sticky enough to cling in bits to the sides of the bowl. Use a spatula to scrape the dough into a lightly oiled bowl, cover the bowl with plastic wrap, and let the dough rise in a warm, draft-free spot for 45 minutes.

(Alternatively, in a food processor combine the yeast, oil, flour, and salt and pulse 2 or 3 times to combine. With the motor running, pour the water into the feed tube and process until the mixture becomes a sticky, wet dough, about 30 seconds. Let it sit in the food processor for 10 minutes and then process again until it becomes glossy and stretchy, an additional minute. Let rise as indicated in the previous step.)

Turn the dough out onto a lightly floured work surface and use a sharp chef's knife to cut it into 2 equal pieces. Coat your hands with flour and gently shape each piece into a round. Let stand on the counter for 20 minutes, lightly draped with plastic wrap.

Heat a panini or sandwich press according to the manufacturer's instructions. Use a rolling pin to roll one of the dough pieces into a rough 10-inch round (don't worry if you can't roll it out to this size). Lift the dough and stretch it across the grids of your panini press. Pull the top down and cook until the pizza bread is light golden with brown grid marks, 2 to 4 minutes, depending on how hot your machine is. Do not overcook. Remove the bread from the press and repeat with the second dough round.

To make 2 grilled sandwiches, simply spread your filling on one pizza bread, top with the other bread, and return to the grill. Grill according to the instructions and then cut into 2 portions with a sharp serrated knife. The breads can also be topped with whatever you like and placed under the broiler for a couple of minutes for quick open-faced sandwiches or pizzas.

All-Purpose FLATBREADS

This simple Afghani-style round can be used to wrap sandwich ingredients, or can be filled and folded in half the way you'd fold a tortilla to make a quesadilla-style grilled sandwich. It's best with softer sandwich ingredients—grilled vegetables, melted cheese, and/or flaked tuna. Chunky ingredients like sausage or steak may tear it. Knead the dough minimally; over-kneading will make it bouncy and difficult to roll into large circles. Wrap leftover flatbreads individually in plastic wrap and freeze for up to 2 weeks. Defrost them on the counter for a few minutes before filling and grilling.

½ cup (114 grams/4 ounces) tepid water (70 to 78 degrees)

1 teaspoon (5 grams/.2 ounce) instant yeast

2 tablespoons (25 grams/.9 ounce) sunflower or canola oil

1½ cups plus 2 tablespoons (250 grams/8.8 ounces) unbleached all-purpose flour

¾ teaspoon (5 grams/.2 ounce) sea salt or kosher salt

Pour the water into the bowl of a stand mixer fitted with a dough hook. Add the yeast, oil, flour, and salt and stir with a rubber spatula just long enough to blend into a dough. With the dough hook, mix the dough on low speed (2 on a KitchenAid mixer) for 1 minute. Turn the speed to medium (6 on a KitchenAid mixer) and knead until it becomes coherent, but is still very soft, about 6 minutes more. Scrape the dough into a lightly oiled bowl, cover with plastic wrap, and let rise in a warm and draft-free spot until it has increased in volume about 1½ times, about 1 hour.

(Alternatively, pour the water into a large bowl. Add the yeast, oil, flour, and salt and stir with a rubber spatula just long enough to blend into a dough. Scrape the dough onto a lightly floured surface. Knead it until it is a smooth but soft—not bouncy—ball, 4 to 7 minutes. Let rise as indicated in the previous step.)

Turn the dough out onto a lightly floured work surface and cut it into 6 equal pieces. Sprinkle with flour and lightly drape the pieces with plastic wrap. Let stand for 30 minutes.

On a lightly floured surface, use a rolling pin to roll one piece of the dough into a thin 9-inch round. Spray a large frying pan or pancake griddle with nonstick cooking spray and heat over medium heat until hot, 2 to

3 minutes. Grill the rolled-out dough until blistered and lightly browned, turning once with tongs, 4 to 7 minutes total. Transfer the grilled bread to a plate and cover with a clean kitchen towel to keep warm. Repeat with the remaining breads.

To use in a grilled sandwich, simply spread your filling on one-half of the bread and fold the other half over the filling to create a half-moon. Grill according to recipe instructions.

Seeded FOCACCIA

MAKES ONE 15 X 11-INCH FOCACCIA, ENOUGH FOR 8 SANDWICHES

Flax, pumpkin, sesame, and sunflower seeds give this bread great richness and texture. A tiny bit of sugar helps to caramelize the crust, but the bread is still wonderfully soft inside, with a moist, cake-like crumb. Press the dough into a sheet pan and, when it's baked, cut it into 8 equal rectangles which, when split, are the perfect size for pressed sandwiches of all types. I use these interchangeably with the ciabatta rolls, but especially love the nutty flavor in vegetarian sandwiches with Italian ingredients, like the Zucchini, Provolone, and Mushrooms (page 118).

2 cups (464 grams/16 ounces) tepid water (70 to 78 degrees)

⅓ cup (50 grams/1.75 ounces) flax seeds

⅓ cup (50 grams/1.75 ounces) pumpkin seeds

⅓ cup (50 grams/1.75 ounces) sunflower seeds

6 tablespoons (50 grams/1.75 ounces) sesame seeds

3 tablespoons (30 grams/1 ounce) olive oil, plus more for oiling the pan and brushing the dough

1 tablespoon (15 grams/.6 ounce) instant yeast

1 tablespoon (20 grams/.8 ounce) sugar

3¼ cups (500 grams/17.6 ounces) unbleached all-purpose flour

1½ teaspoons (10 grams/.4 ounce) kosher or sea salt, plus more for sprinkling

Pour ½ cup (114 grams/4 ounces) of the water into a medium-size bowl and sprinkle the seeds and salt on top. Let stand for 20 minutes to allow the seeds to absorb the water.

Pour the remaining 1½ cups (350 grams/12 ounces) water into the bowl of a stand mixer. Stir in the oil, yeast, sugar, salt, flour, and soaked seeds and mix with a rubber spatula until a rough dough forms.

Use the dough hook and mix the dough on low speed (2 on a KitchenAid mixer) for 2 minutes. Turn the mixer to medium-high (8 on a KitchenAid mixer) and knead until the dough is smooth and elastic, 8 to 10 minutes, scraping down the bowl several times as necessary. It will be quite wet and sticky, and won't clear the sides of the bowl. Scrape the dough into a lightly oiled bowl, cover with plastic wrap, and let rise in a

warm and draft-free spot until doubled in volume, about 1¼ hours.

(Alternatively, in a food processor combine the yeast, sugar, and flour and pulse 2 or 3 times to combine. Scrape the soaked seeds into the bowl. With the motor running, pour the remaining 1½ cups water and the oil into the feed tube and process until a wet dough forms. To knead, continue to process for 30 seconds. Let rise as indicated in the previous step.)

Lightly oil a 15½ x 10½–inch rimmed baking sheet with olive oil. Scrape the dough into the pan and use oiled fingertips to press it into an even layer. If it pulls back from the corners, let it rest for 5 minutes, then stretch the dough again. Brush with a little more olive oil and sprinkle with additional sea salt. Loosely cover the dough with plastic wrap and let stand in a warm and draft-free spot until puffy, about 45 minutes.

Preheat the oven to 425 degrees. Bake the focaccia until golden, about 30 minutes. Transfer the pan to a wire rack and let cool completely in the pan. Cut into 8 squares, split horizontally, and use immediately, or wrap each square in plastic and freeze for up to 2 weeks until ready to use. Defrost on the counter for 15 minutes before using.

Four-Hour BAGUETTES

MAKES THREE 14-INCH BAGUETTES

I learned to make these simple baguettes from my Parisian mentor Basil Kamir when I first started traveling to Paris 20 years ago in search of authentic French bread. Even though it is a staple of the French baking repertoire, it is wonderfully simple to make in the American home kitchen, taking only about 4 hours from start to finish. You don't need any special ingredients or equipment. Professional bakers use a couche, a pleated piece of canvas, to keep their baguettes in shape as they rise, but it is easy and just as effective to use a pleated piece of parchment paper as I explain in the recipe. If you have a baking stone, use it and you will get a wonderfully chewy crust. If not, slide the parchment onto a rimless baking sheet and bake on the sheet. The crust won't be as substantial, but the bread will still be flavorful and full of character.

If you are going to eat your Four-Hour Baguettes on their own, they're best enjoyed on the day they are baked, but day-old Four-Hour Baguettes are just fine when toasted in the sandwich maker. Wrap cooled leftover baguettes in plastic, freeze for up to 1 month, and defrost them on the counter for an hour or two before using.

- 1½ cups (350 grams/12 ounces) tepid water (70 to 78 degrees)
- 1 teaspoon (5 grams/.2 ounce) instant yeast
- 3¼ cups (500 grams/17.6 ounces) unbleached all-purpose flour
- 1½ teaspoons (10 grams/.4 ounce) sea salt or kosher salt

Pour the water into the bowl of a stand mixer. Add the yeast, flour, and salt and stir with a rubber spatula just until all the water is absorbed and a dry, clumpy dough forms. Cover the bowl with plastic wrap and let stand for 20 minutes, to allow the flour to absorb the water.

Use the dough hook of a stand mixer and mix the dough on low speed (2 on a KitchenAid mixer) for 8 to 10 minutes. It will still be a little lumpy, although it will gather into a ball around the hook. Pull it off the dough hook and knead it by hand for a few strokes on an unfloured surface until it is very smooth and springy.

(Alternatively, scrape the dough onto a lightly floured surface and knead with smooth, steady strokes until silky smooth and springy, 10 to 12 minutes. Avoid kneading extra flour into the dough.)

Transfer the dough to a lightly oiled, clear, 2-quart straight-sided container with a lid. With masking tape, mark the spot on the container where the dough will be once it has increased 1½ times in volume. Cover and leave it to rise at room temperature (70 to 75 degrees) for 45 minutes. It will increase by about 25 percent.

Lightly dust a work surface with flour and, using a bench scraper or spatula, empty the risen dough out of the container. Pat it gently into a rectangle, about 6 x 8 inches, and fold it into thirds like a business letter. With the short side facing you, lift the top edge and fold it into the center of the rectangle; lift the near edge and fold it into the center so that it overlaps the top edge by about 1 inch. Quickly slide both hands under the dough and flip it over so the folds are underneath. Slip it back into the container, pushing it down to fit. Cover the dough and let it rise in a warm and draft-free spot until it expands, reaching halfway to the masking tape mark, 45 minutes to 1 hour.

About 1 hour before baking, place a baking stone on the middle rack of the oven and a cast-iron skillet on the lower rack. Preheat the oven to 450 degrees. (If you are baking the breads on a baking sheet, it's only necessary to preheat the oven about 20 minutes before baking.)

Lightly dust your work surface with flour. Uncover the dough and turn it out onto the work surface. With a bench scraper or chef's knife, cut the dough into 3 equal pieces. Gently pat each piece into a rough rectangle and fold it in half. Sprinkle the pieces of dough with flour and lightly drape them with plastic wrap. Let them relax on the counter for 10 minutes.

Cover a baker's peel or rimless baking sheet with parchment paper and lightly dust with flour. Set aside. On a lightly floured work surface, pat the dough into a rough rectangle measuring about 3 x 5 inches. With the longer side facing you, fold the top of the dough down about one-third of the way toward the center. With the heel of your hand, press along the seam using firm but gentle pressure. Fold the bottom of the dough about one-third of the way toward the center and seal the seam firmly. Fold this skinny rectangle in half, bringing the top edge down to meet the bottom edge. Working from right to left, cup your hand over the log of dough and press the heel of your hand down firmly to seal the seam. Dust the work surface with additional flour to prevent the dough from sticking.

To stretch the log, place your hands together, palms down, over the middle of the log. Using light, even pressure, roll the log back and forth as you spread your hands apart. Repeat 3 or 4 times until the log is the desired length, about 14 inches long. Leave the ends rounded.

Place the baguettes on the parchment, seam sides down, about 2 inches apart. Lift the parchment between the loaves, making pleats and drawing the loaves together. Tightly roll two kitchen towels and slip them under the parchment paper on the sides of the two outer loaves to support and cradle the baguettes. Lightly dust the tops of the baguettes with flour and gently drape them with plastic wrap. Let the loaves stand at room temperature for 30 to 40 minutes. They will increase about 1½ times in size.

Uncover the loaves, take away the towels, and stretch the parchment paper out so it is flat and the loaves are separated. Score each baguette with a single-edge razor blade or a serrated knife. Starting from the tip, angle the blade 45 degrees to make 3 slashes about 3 inches long and ½ inch deep.

Slide the loaves, still on the parchment, onto the hot baking stone or rimless baking sheet. Place ½ cup of ice in the hot cast-iron skillet and slide back onto the lower rack to produce steam. Bake the baguettes until caramel colored, 15 to 20 minutes.

Slide the peel or baking sheet under the parchment paper to remove the loaves from the oven. Slide the loaves, still on the parchment, onto a wire rack to cool. Eat them warm or at room temperature. Freeze leftover baguettes in resealable plastic bags for up to 1 month.

2

quick mayonnaises, *pestos,* and other sandwich *enhancers*

There is a reason why mayonnaise and mustard are sandwich staples in the United States and throughout the world. Spreading just a spoonful of one or the other onto bread is the quickest way to add moisture to a sandwich and enhance the flavors of any filling.

When customizing condiments for the sandwiches in this book, I wanted to be sure that they wouldn't call for much more work than reaching for a jar in the refrigerator, while paying off big in terms of flavor. The following recipes won't complicate your cooking, but they will provide wonderful depth and richness to your sandwiches. The panini press intensifies these effects, its heat infusing the other sandwich ingredients with the flavors of Red Pepper–Garlic Mayonnaise or Black Olive Pesto, or whatever you choose to slather or layer on, without any extra work on your part.

In addition to flavored mayonnaises and some wonderful pestos, both of which coat sandwich ingredients with a film of flavor, I've included some of my favorite recipes for vegetable spreads such as baba ghanoush and ratatouille. These chunkier condiments have the added benefit of also providing texture and substance. Spread thickly on bread, they can even become main ingredients.

Some of the best sandwiches combine sweet and savory elements. Slow cooking intensifies the sweetness of Oven-Roasted Tomatoes and Caramelized Onions. The tomatoes are great on an Italian-style sandwich made with thin slices of frittata and cheese, while the onions are terrific with ham and Gruyère. A quicker way to add sweetness is with a fruit compote. I use the Mango Compote on a chicken quesadilla when I'm in the mood for something Southwestern, but I can also imagine it on a vegetarian sandwich with chickpeas and Indian spices. Use my combinations as starting points to design sandwiches to suit your own mood or taste.

Most of these recipes yield more than you'll need for two sandwiches, so you can keep them on hand, alongside your jars of mustard in the refrigerator, for the next time you want to make a quick but satisfyingly flavorful sandwich.

RED PEPPER–GARLIC Mayonnaise

MAKES ABOUT ½ CUP

Roasted red peppers from a jar are not only great on sandwiches but make a wonderfully flavorful spread when pureed and mixed with a little mayonnaise. Use this to enliven everything from grilled eggplant and zucchini to shrimp and leftover chicken.

¼ cup drained roasted red peppers from a jar

1 small garlic clove, put through a garlic press

1 teaspoon fresh lemon juice

¼ teaspoon cayenne pepper

¼ cup mayonnaise

Combine the peppers, garlic, lemon juice, and cayenne in a blender and puree until smooth. Scrape the mixture into a small bowl and stir in the mayonnaise until well combined. This will keep, tightly covered, in the refrigerator up to 3 days.

LEMON-TARRAGON Mayonnaise

MAKES ¼ CUP

I like this mayonnaise paired with chicken, shrimp, and salmon. It also makes very good tuna salad.

¼ cup mayonnaise

2 teaspoons finely grated lemon zest

1 tablespoon finely chopped fresh tarragon

Combine all the ingredients in a small bowl until well blended. This will keep, tightly covered, in the refrigerator up to 3 days.

Lemon-Tarragon Mayonnaise (front), Watercress Mayonnaise, recipe on page 36 (middle), Red Pepper-Garlic Mayonnaise (back).

WATERCRESS **Mayonnaise**

MAKES ABOUT ¼ CUP

Watercress adds a peppery flavor as well as beautiful color to mayonnaise. Substitute arugula (which is a little bit spicier) if you'd like.

- ¼ cup mayonnaise
- ½ cup watercress, tough stems removed, washed, and dried
- 1 teaspoon coarse-grained Dijon mustard
- ½ teaspoon fresh lemon juice

Combine the mayonnaise, watercress, mustard, and lemon juice in a food processor and process until the watercress is finely chopped. This will keep, tightly covered, in the refrigerator for up to a day.

•   •   •

HORSERADISH **Crème Fraîche**

MAKES ABOUT ¼ CUP

I use this with smoked fish, such as trout and salmon, but it is also very good with rare roast beef.

- ¼ cup crème fraîche
- 1½ teaspoons drained prepared horseradish
- ½ small garlic clove, put through a garlic press
- ⅛ teaspoon paprika

Combine all the ingredients in a small bowl until well blended. This will keep, tightly covered, in the refrigerator up to 2 days.

CHIPOTLE **Ketchup**

MAKES ABOUT ¼ CUP

Canned chipotle chiles in adobo sauce have a spicy, smoky flavor that cuts the sweetness of bottled ketchup. The heat of the chiles will vary from can to can, so taste yours before adding them to the ketchup, using more or less according to their spiciness and your taste.

- ¼ cup ketchup
- ½ teaspoon finely chopped canned chipotle chiles in adobo, plus 1 teaspoon of the sauce
- ¼ teaspoon ground cumin
- 1 tablespoon fresh lime juice

Combine all the ingredients in a small saucepan and bring to a simmer over medium heat. Cook, stirring often, until the sauce thickens, 2 to 4 minutes. Remove from the heat and let cool to room temperature. This will keep, tightly covered, in the refrigerator up to 1 week.

•   •   •

BLACK OLIVE **Pesto**

MAKES ABOUT ½ CUP

Just a little of this pesto adds a salty bite to grilled cheese sandwiches made with mild chèvre, mozzarella, or fresh ricotta.

- 2 cups tightly packed fresh basil leaves, washed and dried
- 2 tablespoons walnut pieces or pine nuts
- ¼ cup oil-cured olives, drained, pitted, and coarsely chopped
- 1 small garlic clove, coarsely chopped
- ½ cup extra-virgin olive oil

Combine the basil, nuts, olives, and garlic in a food processor or blender and process until finely chopped, scraping down the sides two or three times as necessary. With the motor running, add the olive oil in a slow, steady stream through the feed tube and continue to process until thick and smooth. This will keep, tightly covered, in the refrigerator up to 2 days.

Quick BABA GHANOUSH

Using bottled eggplant saves the time and hassle of roasting eggplant for this Middle Eastern spread, which is great on panini made with lamb or on vegetarian sandwiches with roasted peppers, onions, zucchini, and your choice of cheese. Look for bottled eggplant in the supermarket, next to the jars of roasted peppers, artichoke hearts, olives, and other antipasto ingredients. The tahini should be nearby.

1 cup eggplant slices packed in olive oil, rinsed, drained, and patted dry

1 tablespoon tahini (sesame spread)

1 teaspoon fresh lemon juice

1 small garlic clove, finely chopped

Salt and freshly ground black pepper

Combine the eggplant, tahini, lemon juice, and garlic in a food processor and process until smooth. Scrape into a small airtight container and season with salt and pepper. This will keep, tightly covered, in the refrigerator up to 3 days.

Quick Baba Ghanoush (front) and
Quick Ratatouille, recipe on page 40 (back).

Quick RATATOUILLE

Most ratatouille recipes call for slow-cooking the vegetables for an hour or more, but this quick version is just as good on a sandwich, and only takes 15 minutes or so on top of the stove. I especially like to use ratatouille to spice up mild sandwich ingredients like chicken or goat cheese.

- 1 tablespoon olive oil
- 1 shallot, finely chopped
- 1 garlic clove, finely chopped
- 1 small eggplant, unpeeled, cut into ½-inch dice
- 1 small red or green bell pepper, seeded and cut into ¼-inch dice
- 1 small zucchini, cut into ¼-inch-thick slices
- 1 medium ripe tomato, cored and diced
- 1 teaspoon red wine vinegar
- ¼ cup finely chopped fresh basil
- Salt and freshly ground black pepper

Heat the oil in a large saucepan over medium-high heat. Add the shallot and cook, stirring once or twice, until softened. Add the garlic and continue to cook until fragrant, about 30 seconds more. Add the eggplant, bell pepper, and zucchini and cook, stirring occasionally, until the vegetables release their juices and soften, about 5 minutes. Stir in the tomato and simmer, stirring occasionally, until the juices have thickened, about 10 minutes. Remove from the heat, stir in the vinegar and basil, and season with salt and pepper. Let cool to warm room temperature and serve. This will keep, tightly covered, in the refrigerator up to 3 days.

* * *

PEAR–APPLE Compote

The sweetness of this simple compote contrasts well with smoked ham, turkey, and sausage. It is wonderful in the fall when there is a bounty of apples and pears and the air is crisp. The aroma quickly fills the house and gathers everyone to the kitchen to see what's cooking.

½ tablespoon unsalted butter

2 Granny Smith apples, peeled, cored, and cut into ½-inch dice

2 Bartlett or Anjou pears, peeled, cored, and cut into ½-inch dice

2 tablespoons light brown sugar

1 teaspoon fresh lemon juice

¼ teaspoon ground cinnamon

Pinch of ground nutmeg

Pinch of salt

Melt the butter in a medium saucepan over medium-high heat. Add the remaining ingredients and cook, stirring occasionally, until the apples and pears are very soft and most of the juices they have released have evaporated, 25 to 30 minutes. Serve warm or let cool, then refrigerate, tightly covered, for up to 2 days. Let the compote come to room temperature before using.

●　　　●　　　●

MANGO Compote

MAKES ABOUT ½ CUP

Alluringly sweet mangoes pair well with spicy and summery sandwiches of grilled chicken and pork.

1 large ripe mango, peeled, pitted, and cut into ½-inch dice

¼ cup white wine

1 teaspoon cider vinegar

1 teaspoon light brown sugar

⅛ teaspoon salt

Combine the mango, wine, vinegar, sugar, and salt in a small saucepan and bring to a simmer over medium-low heat. Cook, stirring often, until the liquid has evaporated and the fruit is soft and beginning to fall apart, 7 to 10 minutes. Transfer to an airtight container and let cool slightly, then refrigerate until chilled. It will keep, tightly covered, up to 1 week.

CHERRY TOMATO Chutney

MAKES ABOUT ¾ CUP

Use this quick chutney when you need some moisture and spice. It jazzes up chicken and turkey and is also very good with shrimp.

- 1 teaspoon olive oil
- 1 teaspoon finely chopped shallot
- 1 cup cherry tomatoes, cut in half
- ⅛ teaspoon ground cardamom
- ⅛ teaspoon turmeric
- ⅛ teaspoon red pepper flakes
- 1 teaspoon fresh lime juice
- 1 teaspoon finely chopped fresh cilantro
- Salt and freshly ground black pepper

Heat the olive oil in a small saucepan over medium-high heat. Add the shallot and cook, stirring, until softened, 2 to 3 minutes. Stir in the tomatoes, cardamom, turmeric, and red pepper flakes and bring to a simmer. Cook until the tomatoes start to soften, 3 to 4 minutes, stirring once or twice. Remove from the heat, stir in the lime juice and cilantro, and season with salt and black pepper. Let cool slightly before using, or refrigerate, tightly covered, for up to 3 days. Let come to room temperature before using.

●　　●　　●

CRANBERRY-ORANGE Relish

MAKES ABOUT ½ CUP

This is a cheerful addition to any sandwich platter. You can increase the quantities to serve it at your Thanksgiving table.

- 1 cup fresh cranberries, picked over and rinsed
- 3 tablespoons sugar
- 1 tablespoon finely grated orange zest
- 3 tablespoons water

Combine all the ingredients in a small saucepan and bring to a simmer over medium heat. Cook, stirring occasionally, until the cranberries pop, about 5 minutes. Transfer to an airtight container and let cool slightly, then refrigerate until chilled. It will keep, tightly covered, up to 1 week.

Cranberry–Orange Relish (top left), Pear–Apple Compote, recipe on page 40, (top right), Cherry Tomato Chutney (bottom).

Oven-Roasted TOMATOES

MAKES 10 TOMATO HALVES, ENOUGH FOR 2 SANDWICHES

Oven-drying concentrates the flavor of tomatoes but still leaves them juicier and softer than bottled sun-dried tomatoes.

   5 medium plum tomatoes (8 to 10 ounces), cored and cut in half lengthwise

   ¼ teaspoon salt

   1 tablespoon extra-virgin olive oil

Preheat the oven to 200 degrees. Set a wire rack over a rimmed baking sheet. Place the tomatoes, cut side up, on the rack and sprinkle with the salt. Roast the tomatoes until wrinkled and shrunken, 4 to 5 hours. Let cool completely, then transfer to an airtight container and drizzle with the oil. They will keep, tightly covered, up to 2 days.

● ● ●

Caramelized ONIONS

MAKES ABOUT 1 CUP

Slow-cooked onions add sweetness and moisture to many sandwiches, especially those containing cheddar, Gruyère, or blue cheese.

   1½ tablespoons olive oil

   2 medium onions (about 1 pound), thinly sliced

   1 garlic clove, finely chopped

   1 teaspoon light brown sugar

Heat the oil in a medium skillet over medium-low heat. Add the onions, garlic, and brown sugar and cook, stirring often, until golden, about 40 minutes. These will keep, tightly covered, in the refrigerator up to 3 days; let come to room temperature before using.

the 3 sandwiches

I've eaten a lot of sandwiches made by artisan bakers as I've traveled through Europe to learn about local breads. They're always a treat, made with handcrafted loaves and filled with local ingredients: fontina, prosciutto, and arugula on Tuscan bread in Florence, knockwurst and mustard on a split Bavarian pretzel in Munich. When these bakers make sandwiches, they're not trying to reinvent the wheel. They're simply making food to nourish themselves when their work is done. Humble though they are, these are some of the most satisfying and memorable meals I've ever had. I really do believe that the best bakers take the same care with their sandwiches as they do with their breads, and because of this their sandwiches are simple but soulful, just like the breads. I'm a baker, too, and I wanted the same natural and easy combinations of ingredients in my own sandwich recipes.

The best grilled sandwiches have an economical design. Every ingredient plays a role in the success of the finished product. Think about classic panini made with mozzarella, tomatoes, basil, and a little bit of olive oil: The cheese provides creamy richness, the tomatoes are juicy and acidic, the basil is fragrant and a little spicy, and the olive oil adds silky moisture and vegetal perfume. Or the Croque Monsieur, with its thin layers of ham and cheese on *pain de mie:* The soft, white sandwich bread that is an alternative to the baguette. The salty, chewy ham is balanced by the gooey cheese, while a little bit of mustard adds some vinegary heat. There are no superfluous ingredients on either sandwich. Every ingredient is essential. In both cases, grilling helps to combine and concentrate the flavors of the fillings.

In every recipe, I have tried to streamline and simplify, instead of getting carried away. That's why my sandwiches have small quantities of meat and rarely have more than three filling components. Any more than this can create flavor chaos instead of harmony. Sandwiches should be satisfying but not overly filling. The panini served at Italian cafés are petite when set alongside the giant submarine sandwiches sold at fast-food restaurants in the United States, but have enough calories to give you energy without regret.

Grilled sandwiches shouldn't require much more time or effort than the average grilled cheese, and I use whatever shortcuts I can to make this possible. For many vegetarian, fish, and seafood combinations, the panini press can do double duty, cooking the fillings before grilling the sandwiches. Large portobello mushrooms cook quickly on the press and make delicious vegetarian burgers when sandwiched on a bun with red onions (also grilled on the press) and cheddar cheese. Asparagus can be grilled before being combined with Taleggio and prosciutto in delicious panini. Shrimp cook on the press in about 3 minutes, before being tossed with a garlicky dressing and layered with arugula and shaved Parmesan to make a grilled Caesar shrimp sandwich.

Panini needn't be reserved for lunch and dinner. This chapter ends with some sweet panini, simple combinations layering mascarpone, almond butter, and fig jam or bread and chocolate, that can be served at breakfast or for dessert. They also make delicious afternoon snacks with a cup of tea or coffee.

It might be tempting to eat your sandwich as soon as it is assembled, but take the time to grill it for a few minutes and you will enjoy it even more. When the filling ingredients are heated, their flavors will become more intense and will mingle in delicious ways. The panini press does more than heat the sandwich ingredients. Just as important, it toasts the bread. Toast, even when made with stale bread, has a deliciously caramelized exterior and a moist interior. Don't be afraid to grill your sandwiches until they are a deep golden, to get these full flavor benefits. But take care not to overgrill, because eventually your bread will burn and dry out. Play with your press to discover the best setting for toasting the bread while heating the filling. After a few tries, you will learn exactly how many minutes it will take to achieve the best result.

Neo-Classic CROQUE MONSIEUR

Most bakeries in Paris also sell bread-based snacks like the croque monsieur, so when I opened my own bakery, I wanted to sell this classic grilled ham-and-cheese sandwich, too, but a more rustic version than the rather dainty sandwiches I had tasted in France, so I used thick-cut ham, chopped cornichons, and grainy mustard to give it some texture and heft. In France, the croque monsieur is most often made with pain de mie (soft sliced white bread), but I often substitute baguette when I want a sandwich I can sink my teeth into. Buy your ham at a specialty foods store where it is roasted on the premises, and have it hand-sliced into ¼-inch-thick pieces.

Four ½-inch-thick slices best-quality country hearth bread or two 6-inch lengths of store-bought or Four-Hour Baguettes (page 27)

2 tablespoons unsalted butter, softened

1 tablespoon grainy mustard

3 ounces Emmenthaler cheese, thinly sliced

6 small cornichons, coarsely chopped

Four ¼-inch-thick slices (4 ounces) baked country ham

Heat a panini or sandwich press according to the manufacturer's instructions.

Spread each piece of bread on one side with 1½ teaspoons of butter. (If using baguette, skip this step.)

Put the bread, buttered sides down, on a cutting board. Spread 1½ teaspoons of mustard on two slices. Top each one with some cheese. Sprinkle the chopped cornichons on top of the cheese. Arrange the ham on top of the cornichons. Top each sandwich with a remaining bread slice, buttered side up.

Put the sandwiches on the press, pull the top down, and cook until they are browned and crisp, 3 to 5 minutes, depending on how hot your machine is. Carefully remove from the press and serve immediately.

GRUYÈRE, SPECK, and CARAMELIZED ONIONS

Speck is a traditional Northern Italian and Southern Austrian air-dried ham similar to prosciutto but less salty. It's worth seeking out for the sake of comparison, and for the most authentic alpine flavor. Gruyère, a classic Swiss cheese, adds a wonderful nutty flavor to the sandwich, and the onions lend sweetness and moisture.

Two 6-inch lengths of store-bought or Four-Hour Baguettes (page 27)

½ cup Caramelized Onions (page 44)

3 ounces Gruyère cheese, thinly sliced

6 thin slices (3 ounces) speck or prosciutto

Heat a panini or sandwich press according to the manufacturer's instructions.

Slice the baguette pieces in half lengthwise and spread some onions on the bottom half of each baguette. Arrange the cheese on top of the onions and drape the speck over the cheese. Top each sandwich with the top half of the baguette.

Put the sandwiches on the press, pull the top down, and cook until they are browned and crisp, 4 to 7 minutes, depending on how hot your machine is. Carefully remove from the press and serve immediately.

COMTÉ, COOKED HAM,
and RATATOUILLE

MAKES 2 SANDWICHES

Comté is a mild cow's milk cheese made in France that melts wonderfully. (Use the slightly more assertive but similar Gruyère if you can't find Comté.) Combined with cooked (rather than smoked) ham and ratatouille on a baguette, it makes a perfect French-style grilled sandwich. If you have leftover ratatouille, this is a great use for it. If not, make my quick version (page 40).

Two 6-inch lengths of store-bought or Four-Hour Baguettes (page 27)

½ cup leftover ratatouille or Quick Ratatouille (page 40)

3 ounces Comté cheese, thinly sliced

8 thin slices (4 ounces) cooked ham such as prosciutto

Heat a panini or sandwich press according to the manufacturer's instructions.

Slice the baguette pieces in half lengthwise and spread some ratatouille on the bottom half of each baguette. Arrange the cheese on top of the ratatouille and drape the ham over the cheese. Top each sandwich with the top half of the baguette.

Put the sandwiches on the press, pull the top down, and cook until they are browned and crisp, 4 to 7 minutes, depending on how hot your machine is. Carefully remove from the press and serve immediately.

PROSCIUTTO, Wilted SPINACH, and CREMINI MUSHROOM PUREE

One of my favorite places in the world is the Campo di Fiori, an outdoor food market in Rome. Every day, vendors of beautiful produce, cheeses, meats, and poultry set up stalls around a big fountain in the center of the piazza. Ringing the market are wonderful little cafés, pastry shops, and the Forno al Campo di Fiori, where I learned to make Roman-style pizza. The owners, cousins Fabio and Bernardino Bartocci, opened a sandwich bar adjacent to the bakery a few years ago and it has been a colossal success, due to simple and elegant sandwiches like this one, made with their signature Italian rolls and baguettes. Here, sautéed mushrooms are pureed to provide flavor and moisture (the Bartoccis use fresh porcini mushrooms, but the more commonly available cremini and even white button mushrooms work well). The baby spinach wilts without overcooking during grilling, and the prosciutto softens up, releasing some of its delicious flavor into the bread. Use sandwich rolls with crisp crusts and fluffy, airy insides, like the ones the Bartoccis bake.

1 tablespoon olive oil

2 cups cremini or white button mushrooms, wiped clean and finely chopped

Salt and freshly ground black pepper

2 Ciabatta Rolls (page 18) or store-bought Italian rolls

1½ cups pre-washed baby spinach

4 thin slices (2 ounces) prosciutto, preferably imported, or Serrano ham

Heat the olive oil in a 10-inch skillet over medium-high heat. Add the mushrooms and cook, stirring occasionally, until they release their liquid and are very soft, about 7 minutes. Transfer to a blender or the work bowl of a food processor. Puree until mostly smooth. Season the puree with salt and pepper.

Heat a panini or sandwich press according to the manufacturer's instructions.

Split the rolls in half. Spread the mushroom mixture on the bottom halves of the rolls. Top with the spinach. Drape two pieces of prosciutto over each portion of spinach. Top each sandwich with the remaining bread slices.

Put the sandwiches on the press, pull the top down, and cook until they are browned and crisp, 3 to 6 minutes, depending on how hot your machine is. Carefully remove from the press and serve immediately.

GRILLED ASPARAGUS, TALEGGIO, and PROSCIUTTO

Very thin, delicate asparagus (about the circumference of a pinkie) can be cooked right on the panini press. If yours are thicker, place them on a baking sheet, brush with olive oil, and roast in a 425 degree oven for 10 to 15 minutes instead. Taleggio is a rich semisoft cheese from Lombardy that melts beautifully and pairs well with both the asparagus and the prosciutto. If you can't find it, any soft-ripened cheese like Camembert or Brie will work.

6 to 8 very thin asparagus spears, tough ends snapped off

2 teaspoons olive oil

Salt and freshly ground black pepper

Two 6-inch lengths store-bought or Four-Hour Baguettes (page 27)

3 ounces Taleggio cheese, sliced

4 thin slices (2 ounces) prosciutto

Heat a panini or sandwich press according to the manufacturer's instructions.

Brush the asparagus with the olive oil and sprinkle with salt and pepper. Place them on the press, pull the top down, and cook until lightly charred, 3 to 5 minutes. Transfer to a plate and let cool slightly.

Cut the baguette pieces in half lengthwise. Spread some cheese on the bottom half of each baguette. Arrange the cooked asparagus on top of the cheese, pressing lightly on them so they adhere. Drape the prosciutto slices over the asparagus. Top the sandwiches with the other halves of the baguettes.

Put the sandwiches on the press, pull the top down, and cook until they are browned and crisp and the cheese is melted, 4 to 6 minutes, depending on how hot your machine is. Carefully remove from the press and serve immediately.

HAM, BRIE, and APPLE FRENCH TOAST

MAKES 2 SANDWICHES

This is a great sandwich for the fall, when local apples are available and you start to crave something warm and filling. Dipped in egg, it makes a terrific weekend breakfast or brunch sandwich. Rich brioche slices are a good choice, but I sometimes use Bread Alone raisin-walnut sourdough bread if I have some left over, for added sweetness.

2 large eggs, lightly beaten

¼ teaspoon salt

Freshly ground black pepper to taste

Four ½-inch-thick slices brioche

4 teaspoons Dijon mustard

6 thin slices (about 3 ounces) Black Forest or other ham

½ apple, cored and thinly sliced

3 ounces Brie, thinly sliced

Heat a panini or sandwich press according to the manufacturer's instructions.

In a shallow bowl, lightly beat together the eggs, salt, and pepper, and carefully dip the brioche slices in the egg to coat.

Carefully place the slices on the panini press and pull the top down. Cook until they are evenly browned, 2 to 3 minutes. Remove to a work surface.

Spread a teaspoon of mustard on each slice of French toast. Arrange the ham on top of two of the slices. Arrange the apples on top of the ham. Arrange the cheese on top of the apples. Top the sandwiches with the remaining bread slices, mustard side down.

Put the sandwiches on the press, pull the top down, and cook until they are browned and crisp, 6 to 8 minutes, depending on how hot your machine is. Carefully remove from the press and serve immediately.

MORTADELLA FRITTATA, FONTINA, and TOMATOES

I love thin frittata as an alternative to sliced chicken or meat. This version, flecked with pink mortadella and chopped parsley, makes a particularly pretty sandwich. It's only in the last few years that Italian mortadella has become available in this country, and if you've never tried it, you must. It may look like American bologna, but it has a luxurious texture and delicate flavor beyond compare.

¼ cup mayonnaise

2 tablespoons finely chopped fresh parsley

1 tablespoon olive oil

¼ teaspoon freshly ground black pepper

4 large eggs, lightly beaten

4 slices (about 6 ounces) domestic mortadella, chopped

2 Ciabatta Rolls (page 18) or store-bought Italian rolls

1 medium ripe tomato, cored and sliced

3 ounces thinly sliced Italian fontina cheese

Combine the mayonnaise and parsley in a small bowl. Set aside. Preheat the broiler to high. Heat the oil in a 10-inch nonstick skillet with an ovenproof handle.

Whisk the pepper into the eggs. Stir in the mortadella. Add the eggs to the hot pan. Cook over medium-low heat, occasionally sliding a spatula around the edges of the pan to loosen the frittata as it sets. Continue cooking without stirring until the frittata is set on the bottom but still loose on top, about 6 minutes.

Place the pan directly under the broiler and cook until the top of the frittata is golden and set, 1 to 2 minutes. Slide the frittata onto a plate to let cool slightly.

Heat a panini or sandwich press according to the manufacturer's instructions.

Split each roll in half. Spread 1 tablespoon of mayonnaise on the inside of each roll half.

Arrange some tomato slices on the bottom half of each roll. Cut the frittata in pieces and arrange them on top of the tomatoes. Arrange the fontina on top of the frittata. Top each sandwich with a roll half.

Put the sandwiches on the press, pull the top down, and cook until they are browned and crisp, 4 to 7 minutes, depending on how hot your machine is. Carefully remove from the press and serve immediately.

CORNED BEEF with MUENSTER CHEESE and WILTED CABBAGE

MAKES 2 SANDWICHES

I learned to love corned beef sandwiches from my grandfather, an Eastern European immigrant who used to take me on weekly trips to the Jewish delis in Buffalo. He taught me to look for corned beef that's not too lean. A little fat makes for a more flavorful sandwich. He also exposed me to handcrafted rye bread from Mastman's deli in the Polish section of town, a bread I've tried hard to re-create at my own bakery. Real rye bread is worth seeking out because it has so much more flavor and character than commercial rye. Commercial rye bread has a beige color and a thin, characterless crust. It is often flavored with artificial caraway flavoring. Real rye bread is made with whole rye flour, so its crumb is darker—gray and brown, not beige. Caraway seeds are kneaded into the dough, and the crust is chewy and thick. My kosher grandfather wouldn't have dreamed of melting Muenster cheese on his corned beef, but I can't resist this combination after having enjoyed it in Germany as an adult.

1 cup thinly sliced green cabbage

¼ cup water

1 tablespoon olive oil

¼ teaspoon salt

Freshly ground black pepper to taste

1 teaspoon yellow mustard seeds

2 tablespoons unsalted butter, softened

Four ½-inch-thick slices rye bread with caraway seeds

1 tablespoon grainy mustard, or more to taste

12 thin slices (6 ounces) corned beef

6 thin slices (3 ounces) Muenster cheese

Combine the cabbage, water, olive oil, salt, pepper, and mustard seeds in a small saucepan and heat over medium-high heat until the water comes to a boil. Turn the heat to medium-low, cover, and steam, stirring occasionally, until the cabbage is very soft and completely wilted, 10 to 15 minutes. Use a slotted spoon to transfer the cabbage to a bowl, leaving any excess water in the pot, and set aside.

Heat a panini or sandwich press according to the manufacturer's instructions.

Spread some butter on one side of each slice of bread. Put the bread, buttered sides down, on a cutting board. Spread mustard on two of the slices. Arrange the corned beef on top of the mustard. Spread an even layer of cabbage over the corned beef. Top with the cheese, then the remaining bread slices, buttered side up.

Put the sandwiches on the press, pull the top down, and cook until they are browned and crisp and the corned beef is warmed through, 5 to 8 minutes, depending on how hot your machine is. Carefully remove from the press and serve immediately.

SAUSAGE, GRAPES, and
GORGONZOLA DOLCE

MAKES 2 SANDWICHES

I had always thought of Gorgonzola as an after-dinner cheese, until I visited the Bartoccis' sandwich bar next to their bakery in the Campo di Fiori, where they spread creamy, mild Gorgonzola Dolce on freshly baked slices of focaccia and served the simple open-faced sandwiches throughout the day. At home, I decided to combine the cheese with sausage and grapes, for a satisfying sandwich made with quintessential Italian foods. The baguette is the perfect shape for the sausage. Here are a few tips for making this sandwich easy to eat: "Butterflying" the sausage and then placing it in one long piece on a piece of baguette ensures that it won't slide out of the sandwich. Likewise, pressing grape slices into the cheese helps them stay put.

One 4-ounce Italian sausage

Two 6-inch lengths store-bought or Four-Hour Baguettes (page 27)

3 ounces (6 tablespoons) Gorgonzola Dolce or other spreadable blue cheese

⅓ cup red grapes (about 9 large grapes), cut into thin slices

Use a sharp chef's knife to cut the sausage almost in half lengthwise, leaving the two halves just barely attached to each other. Grill, broil, or pan-fry the "butterflied" sausage until cooked through. Transfer to a paper towel–lined plate to drain.

Heat a panini or sandwich press according to the manufacturer's instructions.

Slice the baguette pieces in half lengthwise and spread some cheese on the bottom half of each baguette. Lightly press the grape slices into the cheese so they'll stay put. Place a sausage half, flat side down, on top of the grapes. Top each sandwich with the top half of the baguette.

Put the sandwiches on the press, pull the top down, and cook until they are browned and crisp, 4 to 7 minutes, depending on how hot your machine is. Carefully remove from the press and serve immediately.

Sausage, Grapes, and Gorgonzola Dolce

KNOCKWURST with COARSE MUSTARD and PEAR–APPLE COMPOTE

MAKES 2 SANDWICHES

One memorable morning at a suburban Munich bakery, after I watched the bakers pull the night's rye loaves from the oven, I shared their bakers' breakfast of knockwurst with grainy mustard on split Bavarian pretzels, washed down with a glass of beer, of course. Here's my tribute to that sandwich, with fragrant rye taking the place of the pretzels, and the compote providing a sweet counterpoint to the salty sausages (you can substitute 5 or 6 very thin slices of apple for the compote, if you prefer). Use thick slices of bread, preferably a sourdough rye with caraway seeds from a good bakery, for the most authentic German flavor.

2 fully cooked knockwurst sausages

Four ½-inch-thick slices rye bread with caraway seeds

2 tablespoons unsalted butter, melted

2 teaspoons grainy mustard, or more to taste

¾ cup Pear–Apple Compote (page 40)

Heat a panini or sandwich press according to the manufacturer's instructions.

Use a sharp chef's knife to cut the sausages almost in half lengthwise, leaving the two halves just barely attached to each other. Grill the sausage on the press until browned, about 2 minutes. Transfer to a paper towel–lined plate to drain.

Brush each piece of rye bread on one side with the butter. Put the slices, buttered sides down, on a cutting board. Spread two of the slices with the mustard. Spread the Pear–Apple Compote over the mustard. Arrange two sausage halves on top of the compote, trimming the ends if necessary. Top each sandwich with the remaining bread slices, buttered sides up.

Put the sandwiches on the press, pull the top down, and cook until they are browned and crisp, 4 to 7 minutes, depending on how hot your machine is. Carefully remove from the press and serve immediately.

MANCHEGO, CHORIZO,
and CARAMELIZED ONIONS

MAKES 2 SANDWICHES

When made with All-Purpose Flatbreads or store-bought tortillas, these make terrific quesadil-las. With Ciabatta Rolls (page 18) or Italian rolls, they're delicious panini. Manchego is a wonderfully flavorful Spanish cheese similar to dry Jack, which you can substitute if you like. Use cured Spanish-style chorizo, not uncooked Mexican chorizo, here, and cook it briefly before using to render some of the fat.

3 ounces chorizo, thinly sliced

½ cup Caramelized Onions (page 44)

1 teaspoon finely chopped fresh oregano

2 All-Purpose Flatbreads (page 22) or store-bought 8-inch round flour tortillas or flatbreads

3 ounces Manchego cheese, thinly sliced

Heat a panini or sandwich press according to the manufacturer's instructions.

Heat a medium skillet over medium heat and add the chorizo. Cook until it releases some fat and begins to brown, 2 to 3 minutes. Use a slotted spoon to transfer to a paper towel–lined plate.

Combine the onions and oregano in a small bowl.

Arrange the onions on one-half of each flatbread. Arrange the chorizo on top of the onions. Arrange the cheese on top of the chorizo. Fold the flatbreads over.

Put the sandwiches on the press, pull the top down, and cook until they are browned and crisp, 3 to 6 minutes, depending on how hot your machine is. Carefully remove from the press and serve immediately.

GOAT CHEESE with SALAMI
and BLACK OLIVE PESTO

MAKES 2 SANDWICHES

The star of this sandwich is the fresh-tasting, tangy goat cheese. I buy mine from Coach Farm, which is only a few miles away from me in the Hudson Valley. Thin slices of salami draped over the cheese are like a condiment, adding flavor and spice but not too much salt. I prefer Italian salamis to American ones, because they are not as fatty and have more flavor and spice.

2 squares Seeded Focaccia (page 24) or store-bought seeded Italian rolls

1 tablespoon Black Olive Pesto (page 37)

3 ounces fresh goat cheese

6 thin slices (about 1 ounce) aged salami

Heat a panini or sandwich press according to the manufacturer's instructions.

Split the bread in half with a serrated knife. Spread the bottom half of each with 1½ teaspoons of the pesto. Spread the goat cheese on top of the pesto. Drape the salami over the goat cheese. Place the top halves of the bread on the salami.

Put the sandwiches on the press, pull the top down, and cook until the cheese is melted and the bread is golden, 3 to 6 minutes, depending on how hot your machine is. Carefully remove from the press and serve immediately.

Catskills CUBANO

An authentic Cuban sandwich has roast pork, ham, Swiss cheese, pickles, and mustard, and I don't deviate much from this formula. I like Serrano ham or prosciutto instead of the traditional cured ham. To add a little heat, I substitute chopped pickled jalapeños for the pickles. I also like them on ciabatta rolls, although any soft rolls or soft baguette will do. Use leftover sliced pork tenderloin or roast pork from the prepared foods section of the supermarket.

2 Ciabatta Rolls (page 18), store-bought Italian rolls, or 6-inch lengths of soft Italian bread

2 tablespoons yellow mustard

4 thin slices (about 2 ounces) Swiss cheese

2 teaspoons finely chopped pickled jalapeños or more to taste

4 thin slices (about 2 ounces) Serrano ham, prosciutto, or cured ham

4 thin slices (about 2 ounces) roast pork

Heat a panini or sandwich press according to the manufacturer's instructions.

Split the rolls in half with a serrated knife. Spread 1 tablespoon of mustard over the cut side of the bottom half of each roll. Place a slice of cheese on top of the mustard. Sprinkle with the pickled jalapeños. Lay 2 slices of ham over the jalapeños. Arrange the pork on top of the ham. Top with the top halves of the rolls.

Put the sandwiches on the press, pull the top down, and cook until they are browned and crisp, 4 to 7 minutes, depending on how hot your machine is. Carefully remove from the press and serve immediately.

Grilled ITALIAN HERO SANDWICH

A meaty hero sandwich is wonderful when pressed and grilled. Warmed up, the deli ingredients just taste better. Try to find mortadella imported from Italy. It's got a texture and flavor that American brands (which taste more like bologna) don't have. Imported prosciutto and provolone will also improve the quality of the sandwich. Use a thick, hearty baguette or Italian loaf to hold the generous fillings, and don't skip the hot peppers and peppery arugula, which cut the richness of the meats and cheese.

Two 6-inch lengths store-bought or Four-Hour Baguettes (page 27)

¼ cup extra-virgin olive oil

1 tablespoon red wine vinegar

1 cup arugula, washed and dried

¼ cup thinly sliced peperoncini

2 thin slices (2 ounces) domestic mortadella

4 thin slices (2 ounces) prosciutto

6 thin slices (2 ounces) hot or sweet soppressata

4 thin slices (4 ounces) provolone cheese

Heat a panini or sandwich press according to the manufacturer's instructions.

Slice the baguette pieces in half lengthwise with a serrated knife. Brush the insides with the oil and vinegar. Lay the bread, cut sides up, on a work surface. Arrange the arugula and then the peppers on the bottom halves. Drape the mortadella, prosciutto, and soppressata on top of the vegetables. Top with the provolone. Top each sandwich with the top half of each baguette.

Put the sandwiches on the press, pull the top down, and cook until they are browned and crisp and the cheese is melted, 5 to 7 minutes, depending on how hot your machine is. Carefully remove from the press and serve immediately.

LAMB, EGGPLANT, and FETA CHEESE

MAKES 2 SANDWICHES

When my daughter Liv, who is an excellent cook, came back from a period of graduate studies in the Middle East, she sparked my interest in the foods popular in the Eastern Mediterranean, among them lamb, feta cheese, and garlicky eggplant. When I have leftover slices of leg of lamb, I always treat myself to this sandwich. Let the meat stand on the counter for 15 minutes to come to room temperature before assembling the sandwiches, so the filling isn't icy cold when you put them in the panini press. And make sure to slice the lamb very thin, for easy eating. If you have leftover grilled eggplant, you can use that in place of the baba ghanoush, or simply use the bottled eggplant if you'd like.

2 All-Purpose Flatbreads (page 22) or pita breads

1 tablespoon olive oil

⅓ cup Quick Baba Ghanoush (page 38)

8 thin slices (about 4 ounces) leg of lamb

½ cup (about 2 ounces) crumbled feta cheese

1 tablespoon finely chopped fresh parsley

Heat a panini or sandwich press according to the manufacturer's instructions.

If using pita breads, slice them in half with a serrated knife. Brush both sides of the flatbreads or pita breads with the olive oil.

Spread some baba ghanoush on one side of each flatbread or on the bottom halves of the pita breads. Arrange the sliced lamb on top of the baba ghanoush. Sprinkle the feta cheese over the lamb and sprinkle the parsley on top of the feta. Fold over the flatbreads to cover the filling, or top with the top halves of the pita breads.

Put the sandwiches on the press, pull the top down, and cook until they are browned and crisp, 4 to 7 minutes, depending on how hot your machine is. Carefully remove from the press and serve immediately.

ROAST BEEF with
BLUE CHEESE and BACON

Gorgonzola Dolce is a wonderfully mild blue cheese that pairs perfectly with rare roast beef and crisp bacon. I like the sandwiches only lightly toasted because the cheese needs just a little heat to melt beautifully, and the roast beef tastes best still a little chilled from the refrigerator. Whenever I buy a pound of nitrate-free bacon at my local smokehouse, I separate it into 4-slice portions, wrap them in plastic, and freeze them so when I want to make a sandwich I have the small amount of bacon I need. Defrost the bacon on the countertop for 20 minutes before cooking it on the press.

4 slices bacon

2 Ciabatta Rolls (page 18) or 2 store-bought Italian rolls

2 ounces (about 4 tablespoons) Gorgonzola Dolce or other spreadable blue cheese

8 thin slices (about 4 ounces) rare roast beef

Freshly ground black pepper to taste

Heat a panini or sandwich press according to the manufacturer's instructions. Cook the bacon in the press until crisp, 5 to 8 minutes. Transfer to a paper towel–lined plate to cool slightly.

Split the rolls in half with a serrated knife. Spread the bottom half of each roll with the Gorgonzola Dolce. Arrange the roast beef on top of the cheese and sprinkle with black pepper. Arrange the bacon on top of the roast beef. Place the top halves of the rolls on top of the bacon.

Put the sandwiches on the press, pull the top down, and cook until the cheese is just melted and the outsides of the rolls are warmed, 2 to 4 minutes. Carefully remove from the press and serve immediately.

FILET MIGNON with MUSHROOMS and RED PEPPER–GARLIC MAYONNAISE

MAKES 2 SANDWICHES

Filet mignon makes a simple but luxurious steak sandwich, especially with the addition of mushrooms and Red Pepper–Garlic Mayonnaise. I like my filet mignon very rare, and when I grill thin slices of it right on the panini press, they cook beautifully. So much better than using leftovers!

2 tablespoons olive oil

2 cups cremini or white button mushrooms, wiped clean and finely chopped

Salt and freshly ground black pepper to taste

½ pound filet mignon, cut into ⅓-inch-thick slices

2 Ciabatta Rolls (page 18) or store-bought Italian rolls

3 tablespoons Red Pepper–Garlic Mayonnaise (page 34)

½ cup baby arugula, washed and dried

Heat 1 tablespoon of olive oil in a medium skillet over medium-high heat. Add the mushrooms and cook, stirring occasionally, until they release their liquid and are very soft, about 7 minutes. Season with salt and pepper and set aside to cool slightly.

Heat a panini or sandwich press according to the manufacturer's instructions.

Brush the filet pieces with the remaining 1 tablespoon of olive oil and sprinkle with salt and pepper. Lay them on the panini press, pull the top down, and grill until seared on the outside but rare on the inside, 3 to 4 minutes.

While the steak is cooking, split the rolls in half and spread 1½ tablespoons of the mayonnaise on the bottom half of each one. Arrange the mushrooms on top of the mayonnaise. Arrange the arugula on top of the mushrooms. Lay the steak slices on top of the arugula. Top each sandwich with the remaining roll halves.

Put the sandwiches on the press, pull the top down, and cook until they are browned and crisp, 3 to 6 minutes, depending on how hot your machine is. Carefully remove from the press and serve immediately.

Smoked TURKEY, AVOCADO, and CHERRY TOMATO Chutney

MAKES 2 SANDWICHES

We created this sandwich at the Bread Alone Café to use with the organic, antibiotic-free smoked turkey we get from a nearby turkey farm in upstate New York. The Indian flavors in the chutney give the turkey an exotic flavor appreciated by my customers, and the avocado adds nutritious creaminess to the sandwich. Quesido is a soft Mexican-style cheese that melts easily and has a mild, creamy flavor. If you can't find it, substitute fresh mozzarella cheese.

2 squares Seeded Focaccia (page 24) or four ½-inch-thick slices whole-grain seeded bread

¼ cup Cherry Tomato Chutney (page 42)

1 small avocado, peeled, pitted, and thinly sliced

1 teaspoon fresh lime juice

6 thin slices (3 ounces) smoked turkey

3 ounces quesido or fresh mozzarella cheese, thinly sliced

Heat a panini or sandwich press according to the manufacturer's instructions.

Slice the focaccia in half with a serrated knife. Spread the bottom halves of the focaccia squares with the chutney. Arrange the avocado slices on top of the chutney. Sprinkle the avocado with the lime juice. Arrange the turkey on top of the avocado and the cheese on top of the turkey. Top each sandwich with a focaccia half.

Put the sandwiches on the press, pull the top down, and cook until they are browned and crisp, 4 to 7 minutes, depending on how hot your machine is. Carefully remove from the press and serve immediately.

TURKEY and STILTON Sandwiches with CRANBERRY–ORANGE Relish

MAKES 2 SANDWICHES

This is my day-after-Thanksgiving sandwich, using leftover turkey, cranberry relish, and crumbled Stilton left over from the cheese course.

1 cup (about 4 ounces) crumbled Stilton or other crumbly blue cheese

2 tablespoons mayonnaise

Four ½-inch-thick slices country hearth bread

12 thin slices (6 ounces) turkey

½ cup Cranberry–Orange Relish (page 42) or any cranberry sauce or relish

Heat a panini or sandwich press according to the manufacturer's instructions.

Combine the Stilton and mayonnaise in a small bowl and stir until well blended.

Spread the cheese mixture on two of the slices of bread. Top with the turkey. Spoon the relish on top of the turkey. Top with the remaining slices of bread.

Put the sandwiches on the press, pull the top down, and cook until they are browned and crisp, 4 to 7 minutes, depending on how hot your machine is. Carefully remove from the press and serve immediately.

TURKEY with BACON, WATERCRESS MAYONNAISE, and AGED CHEDDAR

Watercress mayonnaise and aged cheddar cheese revivify the standard turkey and bacon combination. You don't have to spend a fortune on the cheese, but do seek out cheddar from large producers such as Cabot, who hold onto some of their cheeses for 18 months or longer to give them character and bite.

4 slices thick-cut bacon, preferably apple-smoked

3 tablespoons Watercress Mayonnaise (page 36) or more to taste

Four ½-inch-thick slices rye or whole wheat bread

½ cup watercress, tough stems trimmed, washed, and dried

8 thin slices (4 ounces) turkey breast

2 ounces best-quality aged cheddar cheese, thinly sliced

Cook the bacon until crisp but not dry. (You can do this directly on the press, in a pan, or in the microwave). Drain on paper towels. Cut each slice in half so you have 8 short pieces.

Heat a panini or sandwich press according to the manufacturer's instructions.

Spread some mayonnaise on each slice of bread. Arrange the watercress on top of the mayonnaise. Arrange the turkey on top of the watercress. Lay the bacon on top of the turkey. Arrange the cheddar slices on top of the bacon. Top each sandwich with a piece of the remaining bread, mayonnaise side down.

Put the sandwiches on the press, pull the top down, and cook until they are browned and crisp and the cheese is melted, 5 to 7 minutes, depending on how hot your machine is. Carefully remove from the press and serve immediately.

CHICKEN with FRESH RICOTTA and MANGO COMPOTE

MAKES 2 SANDWICHES

This filling is too chunky to be contained in a tortilla or flatbread, so use a Pizza Bread or crusty roll instead. The chicken and mango have a Mexican flavor, with the fresh ricotta standing in for mild queso fresco, which can be difficult to find. Fresh ricotta, especially the kind made at an Italian deli, can be watery. Let it stand in a strainer for 15 minutes to allow the excess moisture to drain off before using it in a sandwich.

½ cup fresh ricotta cheese, preferably handmade

2 Grilled Pizza Breads (page 20) or 2 crusty rolls

1½ cups (about 8 ounces) shredded grilled chicken

½ cup Mango Compote (page 41) or 2 tablespoons store-bought mango chutney

Place the ricotta cheese in a fine strainer. Set the strainer over a bowl and let stand, stirring occasionally, for 15 minutes.

Heat a panini or sandwich press according to the manufacturer's instructions.

Place one pizza bread on a work surface and arrange the chicken on top of it, or slice the rolls in half and arrange the chicken on the bottom half of each roll. Spoon the Mango Compote on top of the chicken. Spoon the drained ricotta cheese on top of the compote. Top with the remaining pizza bread or top each sandwich with the top half of the roll.

Put the filled pizza bread or sandwiches on the press, pull the top down, and cook until they are browned and crisp, 4 to 7 minutes, depending on how hot your machine is. Carefully remove from the press. Use a sharp serrated knife to slice the large pizza sandwich in half. Serve immediately.

CHICKEN and RICOTTA SALATA with CUCUMBER–TOMATO Salad

MAKES 2 SANDWICHES

Use this summery recipe when you have leftover grilled chicken. You can take the Middle Eastern combination of cucumber, tomato, and mint even further by using All-Purpose Flatbreads here, although focaccia rolls will still give the sandwiches a Mediterranean flavor. Ricotta salata is less salty than most feta cheese, but still has plenty of salt to season the sandwiches. But if you love feta, feel free to use it here. Make sure to grate or crumble the cheese, because it won't melt otherwise. Seed the cucumbers and tomatoes, so they don't drench the sandwiches with liquid.

½ cup peeled, seeded, and finely chopped cucumber (about ½ small cucumber)

½ cup seeded and finely chopped tomato (about 1 large tomato)

1 tablespoon finely chopped fresh mint

1 tablespoon extra-virgin olive oil

1 teaspoon fresh lemon juice

Salt and freshly ground black pepper to taste

2 All-Purpose Flatbreads (page 22), Ciabatta Rolls (page 18), or store-bought flatbreads

1 cup (about 5 ounces) shredded grilled chicken

½ cup (about 2 ounces) grated ricotta salata or feta cheese

Heat a panini or sandwich press according to the manufacturer's instructions.

Combine the cucumber, tomato, mint, olive oil, lemon juice, salt, and pepper to taste in a small bowl. Be careful not to oversalt the salad, as the cheese has plenty of salt.

If using flatbreads, arrange the chicken on one-half of each flatbread. If using rolls, slice the rolls in half and arrange the chicken on the bottom half of each roll. Spoon the cucumber-tomato salad in an even layer over the chicken. Sprinkle with the ricotta salata. Fold the flatbreads over or top each sandwich with the remaining roll halves.

Put the sandwiches on the press, pull the top down, and cook until they are browned and crisp, 4 to 7 minutes, depending on how hot your machine is. Carefully remove from the press and serve immediately.

Smoked CHICKEN, ST. ANDRÉ, and PEAR–APPLE COMPOTE

MAKES 2 SANDWICHES

I love the combination of the smoky chicken and the sweet fruit compote here. The triple crème cheese (substitute Brie or Exploratuer if you like) adds a creamy component, balancing the acidity of the fruit. You can also substitute 5 or 6 thin slices of apple for the compote, if you prefer.

Two 6-inch-lengths store-bought or Four-Hour Baguettes (page 27)

2 tablespoons grainy mustard

4 ounces St. André or other triple crème cheese

12 thin slices (6 ounces) smoked chicken

¾ cup Pear–Apple Compote (page 40)

Heat a panini or sandwich press according to the manufacturer's instructions.

Slice the baguette pieces in half lengthwise. Spread some mustard on the bottom half of each baguette. Spread some cheese on top of the mustard. Arrange the smoked chicken on top of the cheese. Spoon the compote on top of the chicken. Top each sandwich with the top half of the baguette.

Put the sandwiches on the press, pull the top down, and cook until they are browned and crisp, 4 to 7 minutes, depending on how hot your machine is. Carefully remove from the press and serve immediately.

CHICKEN with LEMON–TARRAGON MAYONNAISE and RED GRAPES

MAKES 2 SANDWICHES

When I have leftover roast chicken, I shred it and use it in this simple but wildly flavorful sandwich. Red grapes add pretty color, but use green if that's what you have on hand.

1½ cups (about 8 ounces) shredded roast chicken

¼ cup Lemon–Tarragon Mayonnaise (page 34)

Salt and freshly ground black pepper to taste

Two 6-inch lengths store-bought or Four-Hour Baguettes (page 27)

½ cup red seedless grapes, cut in half

Heat a panini or sandwich press according to the manufacturer's instructions.

Combine the chicken and mayonnaise in a medium bowl and stir to coat. Season with salt and pepper.

Slice the baguette pieces in half lengthwise and arrange the grapes in a single layer on the bottom half of each baguette. Spoon the chicken mixture on top of the grapes. Top each sandwich with the top half of the baguette.

Put the sandwiches on the press, pull the top down, and cook until they are browned and crisp, 4 to 7 minutes, depending on how hot your machine is. Carefully remove from the press and serve immediately.

BARBECUED CHICKEN with
BLUE CHEESE and CELERY

MAKES 2 SANDWICHES

I grew up in Buffalo, and this sandwich is a tribute to my hometown's favorite chicken wing recipe. If you don't have any leftover barbecued chicken, plain cooked chicken will do, especially when tossed with spicy barbecue sauce. For easy eating, peel away the toughest outer layer of strings from your celery stalk and slice very thin. I use ciabatta rolls or other large square or round rolls (rather than baguette) to contain the rather messy filling.

1½ cups (about 8 ounces) shredded barbecued chicken

3 tablespoons barbecue sauce (optional)

¼ cup mayonnaise

2 tablespoons sour cream

⅓ cup crumbled blue cheese

1 scallion (white and light green parts), finely chopped

Salt and freshly ground black pepper to taste

2 Ciabatta Rolls (page 18) or store-bought Italian rolls

1 celery stalk, trimmed, tough outer strings peeled away, and thinly sliced

Heat a panini or sandwich press according to the manufacturer's instructions.

Combine the chicken and barbecue sauce, if using, in a small bowl and stir to coat.

Make the blue cheese dressing: Combine the mayonnaise, sour cream, blue cheese, and scallion in a small bowl and stir to combine. Season with salt and pepper.

Slice the rolls in half and spread some blue cheese dressing on the inside of each roll. Arrange the sliced celery on the bottom halves of the rolls. Pile the chicken on top of the celery. Top each sandwich with the top half of the roll.

Put the sandwiches on the press, pull the top down, and cook until they are brown and crisp, 4 to 7 minutes, depending on how hot your machine is. Carefully remove from the press and serve immediately.

TUSCAN CHICKEN with
ARTICHOKES and WHITE BEANS

MAKES 2 SANDWICHES

I've gathered some of my favorite Tuscan ingredients and flavors—rosemary, artichokes, white beans, olive oil—to make this comforting chicken sandwich. Use leftover grilled chicken, buy grilled chicken breasts at the deli counter of your supermarket, or grill a boneless chicken breast just for the sandwich. It will be well worth your time.

¼ cup mayonnaise

½ small garlic clove, put through a garlic press

1 teaspoon fresh lemon juice

½ teaspoon finely chopped fresh rosemary

1½ cups (about 8 ounces) shredded roast chicken

1 cup canned white beans, drained and rinsed

2 tablespoons olive oil

Salt and freshly ground black pepper to taste

2 squares Seeded Focaccia (page 24) or seeded Italian rolls

⅔ cup bottled artichoke hearts, drained and sliced

Heat a panini or sandwich press according to the manufacturer's instructions.

Combine the mayonnaise, garlic, lemon juice, and rosemary in a medium bowl. Add the chicken and toss to coat.

Combine the beans and olive oil in a blender or the work bowl of a food processor and blend until smooth, scraping down the sides of the blender or bowl once or twice as necessary. Scrape into a small bowl and season with salt and pepper.

Slice the focaccia or rolls in half lengthwise and spread the bean puree on the bottom half of each baguette. Spoon the chicken mixture on top of the puree. Top with the artichoke slices and the remaining focaccia halves.

Put the sandwiches on the press, pull the top down, and cook until they are browned and crisp, 4 to 7 minutes, depending on how hot your machine is. Carefully remove from the press and serve immediately.

Grilled CHICKEN and ASIAN SLAW

MAKES 2 SANDWICHES

Creamy peanut butter is a good binder for sandwich ingredients with Asian flavors. I like to top this carrot-and-cabbage slaw with leftover grilled chicken, but sautéed or broiled tofu also works well.

1 teaspoon soy sauce

2 teaspoons rice vinegar

½ teaspoon toasted sesame oil

1½ tablespoons creamy peanut butter

½ teaspoon peeled and finely chopped fresh ginger

1 tablespoon finely chopped fresh cilantro

¼ teaspoon sugar

1½ cups thinly sliced green cabbage

1 medium carrot, grated

2 All-Purpose Flatbreads (page 22), Ciabatta Rolls (page 18), or store-bought flatbreads

1½ cups (about 8 ounces) shredded grilled chicken

Heat a panini or sandwich press according to the manufacturer's instructions.

Whisk together the soy sauce, vinegar, sesame oil, peanut butter, ginger, cilantro, and sugar in a medium bowl. Add the cabbage and carrot and stir to coat.

Arrange the slaw on half of each flatbread or the bottom half of each roll. Spoon the chicken in an even layer over the slaw. Fold the flatbreads over the filling or top each sandwich with the other half of the roll.

Put the sandwiches on the press, pull the top down, and cook until they are browned and crisp, 4 to 7 minutes, depending on how hot your machine is. Carefully remove from the press and serve immediately.

DUCK CONFIT with APRICOT JAM, DIJON MUSTARD, and SHAVED FENNEL

When I first tasted duck confit, in cooking school, I fell in love with it. It is wonderfully rich and fatty, but not at all greasy. I have to admit that although I made it many times during my early career as a restaurant chef, I've never made it at home. It just takes too long. That's why I was so excited to see that D'Artagnan, a purveyor of fine poultry and meat products, sells a single fully cooked duck leg weighing about 6 ounces, through many supermarkets and specialty stores and also by mail (see page 140). Now it's possible to prepare luxurious duck confit sandwiches at home in minutes. I like my sandwiches with fennel, apricot jam, and whole wheat bread, all of which help balance the richness of the duck in different ways. Use a mandoline or a very sharp chef's knife to slice the fennel paper thin. If it's cut too thick, it will separate from the sandwich and fall out the sides.

½ small fennel bulb, trimmed and sliced paper thin

2 teaspoons olive oil

½ teaspoon fresh lemon juice

Salt and freshly ground black pepper to taste

1 confited duck leg (about 6 ounces)

2 whole wheat Grilled Pizza Breads (page 20) or four ½-inch-thick slices country whole wheat bread

1 tablespoon unsalted butter, softened

2 tablespoons apricot jam

2 tablespoons Dijon mustard

Heat a panini or sandwich press according to the manufacturer's instructions.

Combine the fennel, olive oil, lemon juice, and salt and pepper to taste in a small bowl and toss to coat. Remove the meat from the duck leg and shred into small pieces. Discard the bone.

Spread some butter on one side of each slice of bread. Put the bread, buttered sides down, on a cutting board. Spread jam on 1 pizza bread or 2 slices wheat bread. Arrange the duck meat on top of the jam. Spread an even layer of fennel over the duck. Spread some mustard on the unbuttered sides of the remaining bread slices. Top each sandwich with one of these slices, buttered side up.

Put the sandwiches on the press, pull the top down, and cook until they are browned and crisp and the filling is warmed through, 5 to 8 minutes, depending on how hot your machine is. Carefully remove from the press and serve immediately.

The Bread Alone TUNA PANINI

I like a good Gruyère even though it doesn't melt as smoothly as processed Swiss or American cheese, because it's been aged properly and has a rich flavor. Best-quality rye bread is essential, for its flavor and chewy texture. The cheese and the bread provide an earthy foil for this fresh-tasting tuna recipe.

One 6⅛-ounce can oil-packed solid white tuna, drained well

⅓ cup mayonnaise

2 scallions (white parts only), finely chopped

2 tablespoons capers, rinsed and drained

¼ cup finely chopped fresh parsley

1 tablespoon fresh lemon juice

Salt and freshly ground black pepper to taste

Four ½-inch-thick slices rye bread

8 thin slices (4 ounces) Gruyère or Swiss cheese

Heat a panini or sandwich press according to the manufacturer's instructions.

Combine the tuna, mayonnaise, scallions, capers, parsley, and lemon juice in a medium bowl. Mash well with a fork to combine. Season with salt and pepper to taste.

Arrange the tuna on top of two of the bread slices. Top with the cheese. Top with the remaining bread slices.

Put the sandwiches on the press, pull the top down, and cook until they are browned and crisp, 3 to 6 minutes, depending on how hot your machine is. Carefully remove from the press and serve immediately.

Asian TUNA PANINI

A fresh-tasting soy and lemon mayonnaise moistens canned tuna, while spicy arugula and sesame seeds provide color and crunch in this out-of-the-ordinary tuna sandwich.

2 Ciabatta Rolls (page 18) or store-bought Italian rolls

One 6-ounce can water-packed solid white tuna, drained well

2 tablespoons mayonnaise

¼ teaspoon soy sauce

½ teaspoon finely grated lemon zest

1 teaspoon fresh lemon juice

2 tablespoons finely chopped fresh mint

1 teaspoon sesame seeds, toasted in a dry skillet over medium heat until golden

Salt and freshly ground black pepper to taste

1 cup lightly packed baby arugula, washed and dried

Heat a panini or sandwich press according to the manufacturer's instructions.

Split each roll in half. Combine the tuna, mayonnaise, soy sauce, lemon zest and juice, mint, and sesame seeds in a medium bowl, mashing well with a fork. Season with salt and pepper to taste.

Arrange the arugula on the bottom half of each roll. Mound with the tuna, then top with the top halves of the rolls.

Put the sandwiches on the press, pull the top down, and cook until they are browned and crisp, 3 to 6 minutes, depending on how hot your machine is. Carefully remove from the press and serve immediately.

ITALIAN TUNA SALAD with AVOCADO and MOZZARELLA

In Italy, tuna is mixed with vinaigrette instead of mayonnaise for sandwiches. Here, I use Italian tuna packed in oil, which is darker and more strongly flavored than regular supermarket tuna, and prepare it this way. Mozzarella cheese and avocado take the edge off the briny tuna and capers, for a perfectly balanced and interesting sandwich.

2 Ciabatta Rolls (page 18) or store-bought Italian rolls

3 tablespoons extra-virgin olive oil

2 teaspoons white wine vinegar

1 teaspoon Dijon mustard

½ small garlic clove, put through a garlic press

¼ teaspoon salt

Freshly ground black pepper

One 6-ounce can imported olive oil-packed Italian tuna, drained well

1 tablespoon capers, drained and rinsed

½ small ripe avocado, peeled, pitted, and cut into ½-inch-thick slices

3 ounces fresh mozzarella, sliced into ¼-inch-thick pieces

Heat a panini or sandwich press according to the manufacturer's instructions.

Split each roll in half. Whisk together the olive oil, vinegar, mustard, garlic, salt, and pepper to taste in a small bowl.

Combine the tuna and capers in a medium bowl. Drizzle the dressing over the tuna. Mix well to combine.

Arrange the avocado slices on the bottom half of each roll. Arrange the tuna on top of the avocado. Lay the mozzarella slices on top of the avocado. Top the sandwiches with the top halves of the rolls.

Put the sandwiches on the press, pull the top down, and cook until they are browned and crisp and the cheese is melted, 5 to 7 minutes, depending on how hot your machine is. Carefully remove from the press and serve immediately.

TUNA, FAVA BEANS, and ASIAGO CHEESE

Here is a tuna and bean combination that is wonderful in a pressed sandwich. Use fresh fava beans when they are in season. The effort of shelling them and peeling away their tough skins after they're blanched is well worth the effort. Out of season, use frozen lima beans, thawed in a colander. Aged Asiago cheese is hard and crumbly like Pecorino Romano, which you may use in place of it if you like.

4 Ciabatta Rolls (page 18) or store-bought Italian rolls

¼ cup extra-virgin olive oil

1 tablespoon red wine vinegar

2 tablespoons finely chopped fresh basil

¼ teaspoon salt

Freshly ground black pepper to taste

One 6-ounce can imported olive oil-packed Italian tuna, drained well

1 cup shelled fresh fava beans, blanched for 2 minutes in boiling water, drained, and skinned, or 1 cup frozen lima beans, thawed

3 ounces aged Asiago cheese, thinly sliced

Heat a panini or sandwich press according to the manufacturer's instructions.

Split each roll in half. Whisk together the olive oil, vinegar, basil, salt, and pepper to taste in a small bowl.

Combine the tuna and beans in a medium bowl. Drizzle the dressing over the tuna and mix well to combine. Arrange the tuna on the bottom halves of the rolls. Lay the Asiago slices on top of the tuna. Top the sandwiches with the top halves of the rolls.

Put the sandwiches on the press, pull the top down, and cook until they are browned and crisp and the cheese is melted, 5 to 7 minutes, depending on how hot your machine is. Carefully remove from the press and serve immediately.

TUNA, WHITE BEANS, and PROVOLONE

MAKES 4 SANDWICHES

I love the creaminess of white beans in contrast with the tuna (mixed with chopped anchovies for extra ocean flavor) in this sandwich. It's such a perfect balance. Just a little bit of melted provolone holds everything together. Using beans is a typically Italian way to stretch one pricey can of imported tuna to make four sandwiches. Economical and delicious.

4 Ciabatta Rolls (page 18) or store-bought Italian rolls

¼ cup extra-virgin olive oil

1 tablespoon fresh lemon juice

2 flat anchovy fillets, finely chopped

Freshly ground black pepper to taste

One 6-ounce can imported olive oil-packed Italian tuna, drained well

One 15.5-ounce can white beans, drained and rinsed

1 tablespoon finely chopped red onion

6 chopped pitted black olives

8 thin slices (4 ounces) provolone cheese

Heat a panini or sandwich press according to the manufacturer's instructions.

Split each roll in half. Whisk together the olive oil, lemon juice, anchovies, and pepper to taste in a small bowl.

Combine the tuna, white beans, red onion, and olives in a medium bowl. Drizzle the dressing over the tuna mixture and mix well to combine. Arrange the tuna on the bottom halves of the rolls. Lay the provolone slices on top of the tuna. Top the sandwiches with the top halves of the rolls.

Put the sandwiches on the press, pull the top down, and cook until they are browned and crisp and the cheese is melted, 5 to 7 minutes, depending on how hot your machine is. Carefully remove from the press and serve immediately.

Smoked SALMON, CHIVE CHÈVRE, and GRILLED VIDALIA ONIONS

MAKES 2 SANDWICHES

I live near Coach Farm, the Hudson Valley goat cheese makers, and I often pair their fresh, tangy goat cheese with smoked salmon instead of using cream cheese from the supermarket. Let your panini press do double duty, grilling the onions before grilling the sandwiches.

½ small Vidalia onion, cut into ⅛-inch-thick slices

1 tablespoon extra-virgin olive oil

1 teaspoon red wine vinegar

Salt and freshly ground black pepper to taste

3 ounces fresh chèvre

2 tablespoons chopped fresh chives

1 tablespoon sour cream

1 tablespoon unsalted butter, softened

Four ½-inch-thick slices dark rye or pumpernickel

4 ounces thinly sliced smoked salmon

Heat a panini or sandwich press according to the manufacturer's instructions.

Brush the onions with the olive oil and place them on the press, pull the top down, and cook until softened and beginning to color, about 3 minutes. Remove from the press and transfer to a small bowl. Add the vinegar, salt, and pepper and stir to combine.

Combine the chèvre, chives, and sour cream in a small bowl.

Spread some butter on one side of each piece of bread.

Place the bread, buttered sides down, on a work surface. Spread some of the goat cheese mixture on two of the slices. Arrange the onions on top of the cheese. Drape the salmon over the onions. Top with the remaining bread slices, buttered sides up.

Put the sandwiches on the press, pull the top down, and cook until they are crisp, 3 to 6 minutes, depending on how hot your machine is. Carefully remove from the press and serve immediately.

SMOKED SALMON with HARD-BOILED EGG and GARLIC MAYONNAISE

MAKES 2 SANDWICHES

Fresh out of cooking school and eager to gain experience in a European kitchen, I moved to Stockholm to work under a famous Swedish chef. The cooks at the restaurant used to make sandwiches for themselves of smoked salmon and hard-boiled egg on dark rye bread. These flavors always remind me of that stimulating time. The garlic mayonnaise, my addition to the recipe, moistens the sandwich and adds a little zip.

1 tablespoon unsalted butter, softened

Four ½-inch-thick slices dark rye or pumpernickel

¼ cup mayonnaise

½ small garlic clove, put through a garlic press

1 tablespoon finely chopped fresh dill

2 teaspoons finely chopped capers

½ cup watercress, tough stems trimmed, washed, and dried

2 large hard-boiled eggs, peeled and thinly sliced

4 ounces thinly sliced smoked salmon

Heat a panini or sandwich press according to the manufacturer's instructions.

Spread some butter on one side of each piece of bread.

Combine the mayonnaise, garlic, dill, and capers in a small bowl.

Place the bread, buttered sides down, on a work surface. Spread some of the mayonnaise on each of the slices. Arrange the watercress on two of the slices. Arrange the eggs on top of the watercress. Drape the salmon slices over the eggs. Top with the remaining bread slices, buttered sides up.

Put the sandwiches on the press, pull the top down, and cook until they are crisp, 3 to 6 minutes, depending on how hot your machine is. Carefully remove from the press and serve immediately.

FRESH SALMON Croque Madame

MAKES 2 OPEN-FACED SANDWICHES

A Croque Madame is a grilled cheese sandwich with a fried egg on top. Here, the soft yolk becomes a delicious sauce for an open-faced sandwich of salmon grilled right on the press sitting on a bed of Swiss chard. This is a great early fall sandwich, when the greens are available locally, and you want something fresh-tasting but hearty.

¼ cup extra-virgin olive oil

1 small bunch Swiss chard or other leafy green, washed, dried, and tough stems removed

Salt and freshly ground black pepper to taste

Two ½-inch-thick slices country hearth bread

1 garlic clove, peeled

2 tablespoons cream cheese

1 tablespoon capers, drained and rinsed

Two 4-ounce salmon fillets, skin removed

1 tablespoon unsalted butter

2 large eggs

2 teaspoons water

Heat 1 tablespoon of the olive oil in a medium saucepan over medium heat. Add the Swiss chard and cook until wilted and soft, stirring occasionally, 5 to 7 minutes. Season with salt and pepper and set aside to cool slightly.

Heat a panini or sandwich press according to the manufacturer's instructions. Brush both sides of each slice of bread with 1 tablespoon of the olive oil. Place on the press, pull the top down, and cook until toasted, 1 to 2 minutes. Rub one side of each toasted slice with the garlic clove. Spread 1 tablespoon of cream cheese on each slice. Sprinkle with the capers.

Brush the salmon on both sides with the remaining 2 tablespoons olive oil and sprinkle with salt and pepper. Place the salmon on the press, pull the top down, and cook until seared and cooked to your desired degree of doneness, at least 3 minutes.

While the salmon is cooking, heat the butter in a medium skillet. Carefully crack the eggs into the skillet, taking care not to break the yolks. Sprinkle 1 teaspoon of the water onto each egg and sprinkle with salt and pepper. Cover the skillet and cook on medium-high heat until the whites are firm and the yolks are still soft, 2 to 3 minutes.

Arrange the cooked greens on top of the cream cheese, place a salmon fillet on top of each bed of greens, and slide a fried egg on top of each piece of salmon. Sprinkle with salt and pepper. Serve immediately.

SARDINES with TOMATO, SWEET ONION, and GRANA PADANA

MAKES 2 SANDWICHES

Sardines have a more assertive fish flavor than canned tuna, which I love, especially in combination with sweet onion and tomato. Grana Padana is very similar to Parmigiano Reggiano, with a saltier and more rustic flavor that stands up to the sardines. You may substitute Parmesan if that's what you have on hand.

1 medium ripe tomato, cored and finely chopped

2 teaspoons fresh lemon juice

1 tablespoon extra-virgin olive oil

Salt and freshly ground black pepper to taste

Two 6-inch lengths store-bought or Four-Hour Baguettes (page 27)

1 cup baby arugula or other baby greens, washed and dried

¼ cup very thinly sliced sweet onion, such as Maui or Vidalia

One 4-ounce can oil-packed sardines, drained well

1½ ounces Grana Padana or Parmesan cheese, shaved with a vegetable peeler

Heat a panini or sandwich press according to the manufacturer's instructions.

Combine the tomato, lemon juice, olive oil, salt, and pepper to taste in a small bowl.

Slice the baguette pieces in half lengthwise and spoon the tomatoes on the bottom half of each baguette. Arrange some of the greens on top of the tomatoes. Arrange the sliced onion on top of the greens. Arrange the sardines on top of the onions. Top with the cheese. Top each sandwich with the top half of the baguette.

Put the sandwiches on the press, pull the top down, and cook until they are browned and crisp, 4 to 7 minutes, depending on how hot your machine is. Carefully remove from the press and serve immediately.

FLOUNDER with SPICY COLESLAW

I was introduced to fish tacos years ago by some of the Mexican-American bakers who work at Bread Alone. Here is my grilled version, with a creamy-spicy coleslaw and sautéed flounder fillets.

2 cups thinly sliced green cabbage

¼ cup mayonnaise

2 tablespoons Chipotle Ketchup (page 37)

¼ cup all-purpose flour

¾ pound flounder fillets, patted dry

Salt and freshly ground black pepper to taste

2 tablespoons vegetable oil

2 All-Purpose Flatbreads (page 22) or 8-inch flour tortillas

1 small ripe tomato, thinly sliced

Heat a panini or sandwich press according to the manufacturer's instructions.

Combine the cabbage, mayonnaise, and ketchup in a medium bowl and toss to coat.

Place the flour in a shallow bowl. Sprinkle the fish with salt and pepper and lightly coat with the flour. Set aside on a plate.

Heat the oil in a large skillet over high heat and cook the fish until golden, about 2 minutes per side.

Arrange the cabbage on one side of each flatbread. Top with the tomato slices and then the fish. Fold the breads over.

Put the sandwiches on the press, pull the top down, and cook until they are browned and crisp, 3 to 5 minutes, depending on how hot your machine is. Carefully remove from the press and serve immediately.

Smoked TROUT, RED ONION, and HORSERADISH Crème Fraîche

MAKES 2 SANDWICHES

I usually don't like to butter my sandwiches before putting them in the panini press, but in this case butter lends richness and flavor to the trout. Horseradish crème fraîche adds moisture and a little bite. Slice your onion very thin, and add just a little to the sandwich so it doesn't overpower the delicate fish.

2 squares Seeded Focaccia (page 24) or store-bought seeded Italian rolls

2 tablespoons unsalted butter, softened

¼ cup Horseradish Crème Fraîche (page 36)

2 paper-thin slices red onion

8 ounces smoked trout, skin and bones removed

Heat a panini or sandwich press according to the manufacturer's instructions.

Slice the focaccia in half lengthwise or split each roll in half. Spread each piece of bread on one side with 1½ teaspoons of butter.

Put the bread, buttered sides down, on a cutting board. Spread some crème fraîche on each slice. Arrange the onions on top of two of the slices. Arrange the trout on top of the onions. Press lightly so the onions and trout adhere to the bread. Top with the remaining two bread slices, buttered sides up.

Put the sandwiches on the press, pull the top down, and cook until they are crisp, 3 to 6 minutes, depending on how hot your machine is. Carefully remove from the press and serve immediately.

CAESAR SHRIMP and ARUGULA

Shrimp grilled right on your panini press are bathed in a Caesar salad dressing. The crisped ciabatta rolls stand in place of the croutons.

¾ pound large shrimp (about 18), peeled and deveined

5 tablespoons extra-virgin olive oil

Salt and freshly ground black pepper to taste

2 tablespoons fresh lemon juice

1 garlic clove, put through a garlic press

2 flat anchovies, mashed

1 teaspoon Dijon mustard

2 Ciabatta Rolls (page 18) or store-bought Italian rolls

1 cup arugula, washed and dried

1 ounce Parmesan cheese, shaved with a vegetable peeler

Heat a panini or sandwich press according to the manufacturer's instructions.

Toss the shrimp with 1 tablespoon of olive oil and sprinkle with salt and pepper. Place them on the press, pull the top down, and grill until cooked through and pink, 2 to 3 minutes. Remove from the press and transfer to a bowl. Let cool slightly.

Combine the remaining ¼ cup of olive oil, the lemon juice, garlic, anchovies, and mustard in a small bowl until well mixed. Pour the dressing over the shrimp and toss to coat.

Split each roll in half. Pull some of the crumbs out to make room for the fillings. Arrange the arugula on the bottom halves of the rolls. Arrange the shrimp on top of the arugula. Drizzle any dressing remaining in the bowl over the shrimp. Arrange the cheese on top of the shrimp. Top the sandwiches with the top halves of the rolls.

Put the sandwiches on the press, pull the top down, and cook until they are browned and crisp, 3 to 6 minutes, depending on how hot your machine is. Carefully remove from the press and serve immediately.

SHRIMP, AVOCADO, and MANGO SALSA QUESADILLAS

MAKES 2 SANDWICHES

Avocado and a little bit of mild Jack cheese provide the creaminess, and mango salsa lends some sweetness and spice to this light shrimp quesadilla.

1 small ripe avocado, peeled, pitted, and thinly sliced

1 tablespoon plus 1 teaspoon fresh lime juice

½ pound large shrimp (about 12), peeled and deveined

1 tablespoon extra-virgin olive oil

¼ teaspoon salt

½ small ripe mango, peeled, pitted, and cut into ¼-inch dice

2 scallions (white and light green parts), finely chopped

1½ tablespoons finely chopped fresh cilantro

½ teaspoon red pepper flakes

2 All-Purpose Flatbreads (page 22) or 8-inch flour tortillas

2 ounces Monterey Jack cheese, grated (about ¾ cup)

Heat a panini or sandwich press according to the manufacturer's instructions.

Place the avocado in a small bowl and sprinkle with 1 teaspoon lime juice. Set aside.

Place the shrimp in a small bowl and add the olive oil and salt. Toss to coat. Arrange them on the press and cook until pink and just cooked through, 2 to 3 minutes. Carefully remove them and set aside. When cool enough to handle, cut them into 1-inch pieces.

Place the mango, scallions, cilantro, pepper flakes, and remaining 1 tablespoon lime juice in a medium bowl and toss to combine.

Arrange the avocado on one half of each flatbread. Arrange the shrimp on top of the avocado. Spoon the mango salsa on top of the shrimp. Sprinkle with the grated cheese. Fold the flatbreads over.

Put the sandwiches on the press, pull the top down, and cook until they are browned and crisp, 3 to 6 minutes, depending on how hot your machine is. Carefully remove from the press and serve immediately.

ZUCCHINI, PROVOLONE, and MUSHROOMS

MAKES 2 SANDWICHES

Finely chopped sautéed mushrooms provide an earthy contrast to the sweet zucchini and mild cheese in this vegetarian sandwich. The long, thin shape of the zucchini dictates the choice of baguettes, but slices of whole grain bread or Seeded Focaccia (page 24) could be substituted easily.

- 3 tablespoons olive oil
- 2 cups white button mushrooms, wiped clean and finely chopped
- 2 teaspoons fresh lemon juice
- Salt and freshly ground black pepper
- 1 medium zucchini (about 10 ounces), ends trimmed and sliced lengthwise into ¼-inch-thick strips
- 3 tablespoons mayonnaise
- 1 tablespoon finely chopped fresh chives
- Two 6-inch lengths store-bought or Four-Hour Baguettes (page 27)
- 6 thin slices (3 ounces) provolone cheese

Heat a panini or sandwich press according to the manufacturer's instructions.

Heat 1 tablespoon of olive oil in a medium skillet over medium-high heat. Add the mushrooms and cook, stirring occasionally, until they begin to release their juices, about 2 minutes. Sprinkle the lemon juice over the mushrooms and continue to cook until most of the liquid has evaporated, 3 to 5 minutes more. Transfer to a bowl, season with salt and pepper, and set aside to cool.

Brush both sides of the zucchini slices with the remaining 2 tablespoons of the olive oil and sprinkle with salt and pepper. Grill on the panini press until soft and browned, 5 to 8 minutes. Set aside to cool.

Stir the mayonnaise and chives into the mushrooms until well combined.

Slice the baguette pieces in half lengthwise and spread some of the mushroom mixture on the bottom half of each baguette. Arrange the zucchini slices on top of the mushrooms. Arrange the cheese on top of the zucchini. Top each sandwich with the top half of the baguette.

Put the sandwiches on the press, pull the top down, and cook until they are browned and crisp, 4 to 7 minutes, depending on how hot your machine is. Carefully remove from the press and serve immediately.

EGGPLANT with ITALIAN FONTINA and RED PEPPER–GARLIC Mayonnaise

MAKES 2 SANDWICHES

I spend a lot of time at the Green Markets in New York City, selling bread. Hanging around with all of the farmers and shopping their stands for produce has helped me learn to cook with an appreciation of the seasons. In August, when small, thin eggplants are available, I take them home and grill them to make this simple but delicious summer sandwich. There's no need to salt and drain farm-fresh small eggplant since it has none of the bitterness of larger eggplant that has been sitting on a truck and in a supermarket for days. If you're using thin eggplants, they conform perfectly to the shape of a baguette. If your eggplants are larger, you may have to cut them after they're cooked to fit onto the bread.

2 small, thin eggplants, or 1 large one (about 12 ounces total), stem ends trimmed and cut lengthwise into ¼-inch-thick slices

2 tablespoons olive oil

Salt and freshly ground black pepper

Two 6-inch lengths store-bought or Four-Hour Baguettes (page 27)

2 tablespoons Red Pepper–Garlic Mayonnaise (page 34)

2 tablespoons thinly sliced roasted red peppers from a jar

4 thin slices (2 ounces) Italian fontina cheese

Heat a panini or sandwich press according to the manufacturer's instructions. Brush both sides of the eggplant with the olive oil and sprinkle with salt and pepper. Put the eggplant slices on the press, pull the top down, and cook until soft and with dark grill marks, 4 to 5 minutes. Set aside to cool.

Slice the baguette pieces in half lengthwise and spread some mayonnaise on the bottom half of each baguette. Arrange the eggplant slices on top of the mayonnaise. Arrange the peppers on top of the eggplant. Arrange the cheese on top of the peppers. Top each sandwich with the top half of the baguette.

Put the sandwiches on the press, pull the top down, and cook until they are browned and crisp, 4 to 7 minutes, depending on how hot your machine is. Carefully remove from the press and serve immediately.

Eggplant with Italian Fontina and Red Pepper—Garlic Mayonnaise

SPICED CHICKPEA SPREAD with TOMATOES

MAKES 2 SANDWICHES

Here is a sandwich inspired by my daughter Liv's cooking. She introduced me to zatar, a blend of spices (usually sumac, thyme, and sesame seeds) popular in the Middle East. It adds unique flavor to this simple sandwich of chickpeas dressed with yogurt. Pureeing some of the chickpeas will hold the sandwich filling together. If you can't find zatar at your local specialty foods store, you can order it online (see Resources, page 138), or substitute a combination of ground cumin and allspice for a different but just as delicious Middle Eastern flavor. Use full-fat yogurt here— low-fat and nonfat yogurt will be too thin and watery. If possible, use imported Greek yogurt, which is deliciously rich and creamy, more like sour cream.

One 15.5-ounce can chickpeas, rinsed and drained

2 tablespoons extra-virgin olive oil

1 small garlic clove, coarsely chopped

2 teaspoons zatar, or ½ teaspoon ground cumin plus ⅛ teaspoon ground allspice

¼ cup plain full-fat yogurt, preferably Greek

¼ teaspoon cayenne pepper

1 small tomato, cored and thinly sliced

2 All-Purpose Flatbreads (page 22) or store-bought 8-inch round flour tortillas or flatbreads

Heat a panini or sandwich press according to the manufacturer's instructions.

Combine about ¼ of the chickpeas, the olive oil, and garlic in a blender or small food processor and process until smooth. Transfer to a medium bowl and stir in the remaining whole chickpeas and the zatar.

Combine the yogurt and cayenne pepper in a small bowl.

Arrange the tomato slices on one half of each flatbread. Spoon the chickpea mixture over the tomatoes. Smooth the yogurt over the chickpeas. Fold the flatbreads over.

Put the sandwiches on the press, pull the top down, and cook until they are browned and crisp, 4 to 7 minutes, depending on how hot your machine is. Carefully remove from the press and serve immediately.

PORTOBELLO MUSHROOMS with GRILLED ONIONS and CHEDDAR CHEESE

MAKES 2 SANDWICHES

Grilled whole portobello mushrooms are a good vegetarian substitute for hamburger, especially when topped with grilled red onions and cheddar cheese. Chipotle ketchup provides acidity and spice, but you may substitute mayonnaise, with maybe a teaspoon of chopped parsley or basil, if you prefer a milder sauce. At Bread Alone, we make our own deliciously crusty Kaiser rolls. Seek out rolls of similar substance, and avoid commercial hamburger buns at all cost.

2 large portobello mushrooms, stemmed and wiped clean

Two ½-inch-thick slices red onion

2 tablespoons olive oil

Salt and freshly ground black pepper to taste

2 round Italian rolls

¼ cup Chipotle Ketchup (page 37)

3 ounces cheddar cheese, thinly sliced

Heat a panini or sandwich press according to the manufacturer's instructions.

Brush the mushrooms and onions with olive oil and sprinkle with salt and pepper. Place them on the press, pull the top down, and cook until softened and browned, 4 to 6 minutes. Transfer to a plate and let cool slightly.

Cut the rolls in half with a sharp serrated knife. Spread some chipotle ketchup on the bottom half of each roll. Place a mushroom on each bottom half. Top with a slice of grilled onion. Cover the onion with cheese. Top the sandwiches with the top halves of the rolls.

Put the sandwiches on the press, pull the top down, and cook until they are browned and crisp and the cheese is melted, 5 to 7 minutes, depending on how hot your machine is. Carefully remove from the press and serve immediately.

ARTICHOKES, Oven-Roasted TOMATOES, and GOAT CHEESE

I associate artichokes with the happy times I've spent at the beautiful farmers' markets in Rome. Fresh artichokes take a little bit of work to prepare and cook. When you don't have a lot of time, or when artichokes are out of season, it's more practical to use bottled artichoke hearts, preferably imported from Italy. In this sandwich, the sweetness of oven-roasted tomatoes contrasts beautifully with the acidity of the goat cheese and earthiness of the artichokes.

- 3 ounces fresh goat cheese
- 1 tablespoon finely chopped fresh basil
- 1½ teaspoons extra-virgin olive oil
- Two 6-inch lengths store-bought or Four-Hour Baguettes (page 27)
- 10 Oven-Roasted Tomato halves (page 44)
- One 6-ounce jar quartered marinated artichoke hearts, drained

Heat a panini or sandwich press according to the manufacturer's instructions.

Combine the goat cheese, basil, and olive oil in a small bowl and mash and stir until the cheese is softened and well combined with the other ingredients.

Slice the baguette pieces in half lengthwise and spread some of the goat cheese on the bottom half of each baguette.

Arrange the tomatoes and artichokes on top of the goat cheese. Top each sandwich with the top half of the baguette.

Put the sandwiches on the press, pull the top down, and cook until they are browned and crisp, 4 to 7 minutes, depending on how hot your machine is. Carefully remove from the press and serve immediately.

MUSHROOM and LEEK FRITTATA with ROASTED TOMATOES and SHAVED PARMESAN

MAKES 2 SANDWICHES

This sandwich is the perfect example of how a few well-chosen ingredients, well handled, combine to make something really delicious and beautiful. Use a crusty country bread, or homemade Pizza Bread (even better) to enclose the firm omelet. A small amount of best-quality imported Parmesan cheese adds a lot of flavor. And take the time to oven-roast the tomatoes (you can do it several days ahead). If you do this once, I guarantee you will become addicted to this method for enhancing their sweetness.

¼ cup mayonnaise

2 teaspoons finely chopped fresh sage leaves

1 tablespoon olive oil

1 leek (white and light green parts), washed well and thinly sliced

¾ cup thinly sliced white button or cremini mushrooms

Salt and freshly ground black pepper to taste

4 large eggs, lightly beaten

Four ½-inch-thick slices country hearth bread or 2 Grilled Pizza Breads (page 20)

10 Oven-Roasted Tomato halves (page 44)

1 ounce Parmigiano Reggiano, shaved with a vegetable peeler

Combine the mayonnaise and sage in a small bowl. Set aside. Preheat the broiler to high. Heat the oil in a 10-inch nonstick skillet with an ovenproof handle. Add the leeks and sauté until softened, about 2 minutes. Add the mushrooms and cook, stirring occasionally, until they release their juices, 3 to 5 minutes. Season with salt and pepper.

Add the eggs to the pan and stir to incorporate the vegetables. Cook over medium-low heat, occasionally sliding a spatula around the edges of the pan to loosen the frittata as it sets. Continue cooking without stirring until the frittata is set on the bottom but still loose on top, about 6 minutes.

Place the pan directly under the broiler and cook until the top of the frittata is golden and set, 1 to 2 minutes. Slide the frittata onto a plate to let cool slightly.

Heat a panini or sandwich press according to the manufacturer's instructions.

Spread the bread on one side with the 1 tablespoon mayonnaise. Cut the frittata in pieces and arrange them on the mayonnaise. Arrange the tomato halves on top of the frittata. Place the cheese shavings over the tomatoes. Top each sandwich with another piece of bread.

Put the sandwiches on the press, pull the top down, and cook until they are browned and crisp, 4 to 7 minutes, depending on how hot your machine is. Carefully remove from the press and serve immediately.

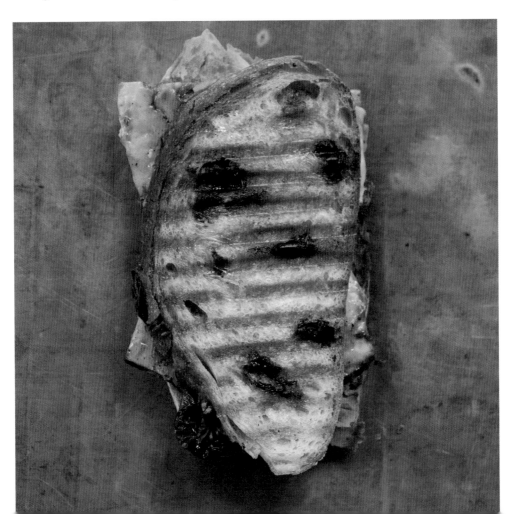

Open-Faced BLUEBERRY and CRÈME FRAÎCHE Brioche Sandwiches

Here is one of my favorite breakfast treats, a slice of brioche, lightly caramelized under the broiler with confectioners' sugar, then topped with crème fraîche, blueberries, and a drizzle of local Hudson Valley maple syrup.

Two 1-inch-thick slices brioche

1 tablespoon unsalted butter, softened

2 teaspoons confectioners' sugar

6 tablespoons crème fraîche

½ cup fresh blueberries, washed, dried, and picked over

2 tablespoons pure maple syrup

Heat the panini or sandwich press according to the manufacturer's instructions.

Place the bread on a work surface and spread some butter on each slice. Sift some confectioners' sugar over each slice. Place on the press, sugar side up, and bring the lid down as close to the slices as possible without touching. Cook until the sugar just starts to caramelize, 30 seconds to 1 minute. Remove from the press and transfer to a plate.

Spread some crème fraîche over each slice of bread. Arrange the blueberries on top of the crème fraîche, pressing down on them lightly so they adhere. Drizzle each slice with some maple syrup and serve immediately.

Open-Faced Blueberry and Crème Fraîche Brioche Sandwiches

BREAD and CHOCOLATE

Here is a recipe for the perfect after-school snack, beloved by children all over Europe. A bit of soft butter spread on the insides of the baguette makes this version luxurious. If you like, you can sprinkle the chocolate with a little bit of sea salt before grilling for a sweet-and-salty effect.

Two 6-inch lengths store-bought or Four-Hour Baguettes (page 27)

1½ tablespoons unsalted butter, softened

2 ounces bittersweet chocolate, broken into pieces

¼ teaspoon fine sea salt (optional)

Heat a panini or sandwich press according to the manufacturer's instructions.

Slice the baguettes in half lengthwise. Spread the butter on the inside of each piece. Place the chocolate on the bottom of the baguettes. Sprinkle with the sea salt, if desired. Top each with the other half of the baguettes.

Put the sandwiches on the press, pull the top down, and cook until they are golden and crisp, 4 to 6 minutes, depending on how hot your machine is. Carefully remove from the press and serve immediately.

MASCARPONE, ALMOND Butter, and FIG JAM

Brioche makes these panini extra rich, but best-quality pain de mie *or white bread will also be delicious. Fig jam is my favorite with the mascarpone and almond butter, but you can use apricot, raspberry, strawberry, or orange marmalade depending on your taste.*

Four 1-inch-thick slices brioche

2 tablespoons unsalted butter, softened

3 tablespoons almond butter

2 tablespoons fig jam

¼ cup mascarpone

1 tablespoon granulated sugar

2 teaspoons confectioners' sugar

Heat a panini or sandwich press according to the manufacturer's instructions.

Spread each piece of bread on one side with 1½ teaspoons of butter. Put the bread, buttered sides down, on a cutting board. Spread 1½ tablespoons of almond butter on two of the slices. Spread the fig jam on the other two slices. Spread the mascarpone on top of the fig jam. Sprinkle with the granulated sugar. Place the almond butter slices, almond butter side down, on top of the mascarpone.

Put the sandwiches on the press, pull the top down, and cook until they are golden and crisp, 3 to 5 minutes, depending on how hot your machine is. Carefully remove from the press, dust with confectioners' sugar, and serve immediately.

Nutella® FRENCH TOAST

Dipping these simple sandwiches of white bread and Nutella, the Italian chocolate-and-hazelnut spread, in egg before grilling turns them into luxurious stuffed French toast. Serve them for a special breakfast or decadent dessert, maybe with some raspberries, sliced strawberries, or sliced bananas and sweetened whipped cream on the side. Watch the sandwiches carefully—you want their outsides to caramelize, but not to burn. If your panini press is not reliably nonstick, spray it with cooking spray or brush it with melted butter before putting the sandwiches in.

Four 1-inch-thick slices brioche

¼ cup Nutella

2 large eggs

¼ cup half-and-half or milk

2 tablespoons confectioners' sugar, plus more for dusting

1 teaspoon vanilla extract

Heat a panini or sandwich press according to the manufacturer's instructions.

Spread 2 pieces of bread with the Nutella. Top each piece with another piece of bread.

Whisk together the eggs, half-and-half, confectioners' sugar, and vanilla in a shallow bowl. Place one of the sandwiches in the bowl and then turn it to completely coat it with the egg mixture. Transfer to a platter. Let stand for a few seconds,

Put the sandwiches on the press, pull the top down, and cook until they are golden and crisp, 4 to 6 minutes, depending on how hot your machine is. Carefully remove from the press, dust with confectioners' sugar, and serve immediately.

Resources

Panini Presses

When shopping for a panini press, look for a very heavy appliance with top and bottom heating elements, a nonstick surface, and a floating hinge that will allow for even grilling of thick and thin sandwiches. Kitchen retailers such as Crate & Barrel (order online at www.crateandbarrel.com or call and order by mail: 800-967-6696), Williams-Sonoma (order online at www.williams-sonoma.com or call and order by mail: 877-812-6235), and Sur la Table (order online at www.surlatable.com or call and order by mail: 800-243-0852) often run specials on good-quality presses made by Villaware and Cuisinart.

Breads

Bread Alone will ship freshly baked artisanal loaves, including a large selection of certified organic sourdoughs, overnight to most places in the United States. To order online, go to www.breadalone.com or call and order by mail: 800-769-3328.

To sample breads from fine bakers around the country, and for famed French sourdough bread from Poilane in Paris, shop at Zingerman's (www.zingermans.com to order or request a mail-order catalog).

Flour

High-quality minimally processed flour is essential for making great bread. For fine flour (including certified organic flour similar to what we use exclusively at Bread Alone), as well as other bread-making ingredients (yeast, seeds) and equipment, go to the King Arthur Flour Company (www.bakerscatalogue.com; 800-827-6836). Giusto's Specialty Foods, a pioneer in milling organic flour for professional bakers for over 20 years, now sells small bags to consumers. To order, visit www.giustos.com or call 650-873-6566.

Cheese

If you can't find Comté, Gorgonzola Dolce, imported Gruyère, or other fine cheese at your local market, order it from one of the country's premier cheese shops, Murray's (www.murrayscheese.com; 212-243-3289).

Chutney

I'm delighted that my friends at Bombay Emerald Chutney Company, who have been selling their wonderful Plum, Mint, Cranberry, and Tomato Chutneys alongside us at New York City farmers' markets for years, are now selling them online at www.bombayemeraldchutneyco.com. These chutneys are an easy way to add exotic flavor to simple grilled sandwiches.

Cured Meats and Confit

D'Artagnan is the place to go for duck confit. They also sell smoked meats you may not be able to buy locally, such as nitrite-free organic bacon, smoked chicken breast, chorizo, and apple-smoked Heritage ham. Order online at www.dartagnan.com, or call to mail-order or request a catalog: 800-327-8244.

Spices

For difficult-to-find spices like zatar as well as more common dried herbs and spices that are uncommonly fresh, order from Penzeys, the midwest spice purveyor. Order online at www.penzeys.com, or call 800-741-7787 to mail-order or request a catalog.

LIQUID/DRY MEASURES	
U.S.	METRIC
¼ teaspoon	1.25 milliliters
½ teaspoon	2.5 milliliters
1 teaspoon	5 milliliters
1 tablespoon (3 teaspoons)	15 milliliters
1 fluid ounce (2 tablespoons)	30 milliliters
¼ cup	60 milliliters
⅓ cup	80 milliliters
½ cup	120 milliliters
1 cup	240 milliliters
1 pint (2 cups)	480 milliliters
1 quart (4 cups; 32 ounces)	960 milliliters
1 gallon (4 quarts)	3.84 liters
1 ounce (by weight)	28 grams
1 pound	454 grams
2.2 pounds	1 kilogram

OVEN TEMPERATURES		
°F	Gas Mark	°C
250	½	120
275	1	140
300	2	150
325	3	165
350	4	180
375	5	190
400	6	200
425	7	220
450	8	230
475	9	240
500	10	260
550	Broil	290

Index